Wild Truth
Bible Lessons

Check out these other great *Wild Truth* books for your middle schoolers!

Wild Truth Journal for Junior Highers, *with companion curriculum* **Wild Truth Bible Lessons** *and* **Wild Truth Bible Lessons 2**

Wild Truth Journal—Pictures of God
The companion student journal to the curriculum you're holding now

Pictures of God

12 wild Bible studies
on the character of a wild God—
and what it means for your
junior highers & middle schoolers

Mark Oestreicher

Youth Specialties

ZondervanPublishingHouse

Grand Rapids, Michigan

A *Division of* HarperCollins*Publishers*

Wild Truth Bible Lessons—Pictures of God: 12 wild Bible studies on the character of a wild God—and what it means for your junior highers & middle schoolers

Copyright © 1999 by Youth Specialties, Inc.

Youth Specialties Books, 300 S. Pierce St., El Cajon, CA 92020, are published by Zondervan Publishing House, 5300 Patterson Ave. S.E., Grand Rapids, MI 49530.

Library of Congress Cataloging-in-Publication Data

Oestreicher, Mark.
     Wild truth Bible lessons—pictures of God : 12 wild Bible studies on the character of a wild
God—and what it means for your junior highers & middle schoolers / Mark Oestreicher.
        p. cm.
     Includes index.
     ISBN 0-310-22365-2
     1. God—Biblical teaching. 2. Christian education of teenagers. 3. Bible—Theology—Study
and teaching—Activity programs. I. Title.
BS544.O47 1999
268'.433—DC21
                                                 99-30185
                                                 CIP

The original concept for this book comes from *52 Ways to Teach Your Child about God*, by Todd Temple (Thomas Nelson Publishers).

The scripts "Amazing Grace Soul Detergent" (Lesson 1) and "The Lemon" (Lesson 3) were written by Andrew Davey of Rossmoyne, Western Australia.

Unless otherwise indicated, all Scripture quotations are taken from the Holy Bible: *New International Version* (North American Edition). Copyright © 1973, 1978, 1984 by International Bible Society. Used by permission of Zondervan Publishing House.

Edited by Laura Gross
Cover and interior design by Patton Brothers Design
Illustrated by Krieg Barrie

Printed in the United States of America

05 06 /VG/ 10 9 8 7 6

To my parents, Dick and Bobbi Oestreicher. A lifetime of thanks for introducing me to the God in these pictures, through your word and deed.

AUG'06 →

Contents

God is like a—

Acknowledgments

Thanks to Todd Temple for encouraging my writing as well as this project. This book is Todd's idea (so send your complaints to him, not me!). Thanks to the awesome product department at Youth Specialties for balancing the delicate duality of our relationship—author and supervisor. Thanks, as always, to my amazing wife and friend, Jeannie, and to our two little nippers, Liesl and Max. You three are the joy of my life.

Does your Bible have photos in it?

Mine doesn't. Just some maps in the back. Photography was invented too late to catch God on film. That's too bad. Some of those Bible scenes would be pretty spectacular to look at. But God didn't give us any pictures of himself. Just a bunch of words.

Strike that. God *did* give us pictures—but he used *words* to draw them. Some are bigger-than-life portraits, others full-motion action shots. Still others are like Hitchcock cameos—blink and you miss him. But if you look close enough, you'll see his picture on just about every page.

In this sense, the Bible is a photo album, brimming with self-portraits of a God who wants to be known. God has put these pictures in the Bible to reveal his *character.* By examining them, we discover who God is and why he's worth knowing better. And we discover something else: who he wants *us* to be. He wants us to copy his picture into our own character.

This book is a guide to 12 God-pictures taken straight from the Photo Album. Here's how the lessons are organized:

Grabs your group's attention to prepare them for what's ahead.

Takes your students into the Bible to catch God in the act of revealing his character.

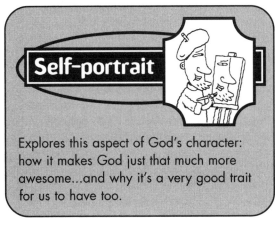

Explores this aspect of God's character: how it makes God just that much more awesome...and why it's a very good trait for us to have too.

Challenges your students to print God's picture into their own lives by living out his character in an immediately practical way.

These lessons are loaded with very creative games, activities, sketches, handouts, and options. But you know your students best—so use what works, and tweak or replace the rest.

If you're looking for a great way to expand your lessons beyond the classroom, check out **Wild Truth Journal: Pictures of God**. This junior high devotional contains short lessons based on 50 God-pictures, including the dozen covered here. On their own, students can continue their discovery and emulation of God's character, even after you've run out of lessons from this book.

By the way, all the books in our *Wild Truth* line (five so far) are written by my friend and fellow junior high fanatic, Mark Oestreicher. If you're not familiar with Mark's style, you're in for a treat. He thinks more like a junior higher than any adult I know. When I read his work, I get the feeling he's writing from a secret location inside a junior higher's head, seeing what the student sees, delighting in a God Sighting in progress. May you experience this same delight as you discover God through the lives of your students. They'll see things we adults keep missing. And if you give them the chance, they may even show them to you.

Todd Temple
10 TO 20 Press

God is like a GiFT

For it is by grace you have been saved, through faith—and this not from yourselves, it is the gift of God. **Ephesians 2:8**

GOALS

Students will—
- Understand why God is like a gift
- Understand how they can be a gift to others by giving themselves
- Write out a plan of action for being a gift this week

Okay, here it is, lesson numero uno. You're ready to dive into this book. Let me give you a few gentle reminders.

1. They're junior highers; you're bigger. (Understand?)

2. They're junior highers, not little adults; the best control you can hope for is controlled chaos. If you disagree with me, you probably shouldn't be teaching young teens.

3. They're junior highers; God is in love with the kids in your group and wants your time with them to be powerful and life-changing. But if you don't *see* the life change, don't assume God isn't bringing it about!

Picture Prep

Gift Exchange

Have a wild white elephant gift exchange (who knows why it's called that?) no matter what time of year it is! Either ask your kids to bring a dorky gift or go to a 99-cent store and buy enough weird and cheap things for each person (make sure they're wrapped). Put all the gifts in a pile in the middle of

You'll need—
- wrapped gifts, one for each kid

the group. Normal white elephant rules are—
- Everyone draws a random number, lowest number chooses a gift, then the next lowest number.
- On your turn, you have a choice to select an unopened gift or steal an opened gift from someone else.
- Opened gifts can only be stolen twice.

You can play with those rules, but you can add a few twists to it.

- Halfway through play, switch directions and have the student with the highest number pick next, then proceed down.
- At some random time of your choosing, everyone with an opened gift must pass it one person to the right (to the next person with an opened gift).
- At some random time of your choosing, every girl, or everyone with an even number, or whomever (be creative) gets to make an additional trade that doesn't count toward the "max of two steals" rule.

After finishing the opening activity, have a discussion about gifts with these questions:
- **What's the best gift you've ever received? Why was it so great?**
- **What's the best gift you've ever given? (It doesn't have to be the most expensive gift you've given.) Why was it so great? How was it received?**
- **If you were going to get the ultimate gift today, what would you hope it would be?**

OPTIONAL DRAMA
Amazing Grace Soul Detergent

Use the drama (page 15-16) to illustrate the gift of God's grace and its effect on our souls. The drama will be best if you have two people rehearse it ahead of time. You could probably get away with using yourself as the announcer and asking another adult or a student (who's a good reader) to wing it. Make sure you have all the props or it won't make sense.

You'll need—
- two copies of **Amazing Grace Soul Detergent** (pages 15-16)
- two semi-prepped actors
- a large bowl on a table
- a white T-shirt and a black T-shirt
- a box of laundry detergent made to look like the skit product

The drama is fairly self-explanatory, so you shouldn't need to ask a bunch of questions to make sure your students understand. You can just move on to the next section of the lesson.

(Important note: I get nervous using *black* and *white* as terms to define sinfulness and purity. I don't want kids to make a false connection to skin color. And I really don't want the African-American kids in my group to feel uncomfortable. But analogy—black and white—*is* found in the Bible. Certainly, the biblical writers, and God himself, never intended to imply one race is sinful and another pure! So be cautious!)

Gift Object Lesson

Ask for two volunteers. Once they're up front with you, pull out two gifts and set them on a table. One should be something cheap like a superball, a set of playing cards, or a pencil. The other should be something

the kids would actually want—like a CD (or a gift certificate to buy one), a whole bag of candy, or a 12-pack of Coke. Whatever the gifts are, it needs to be totally obvious to everyone that the second one is more desirable.

You'll need—
- two unwrapped gifts— one cheap and trashy, one somewhat nicer

Tell your volunteers you're going to flip a coin to see who gets to choose a gift first. But before you do, explain that there's a little more to this. If they choose the first gift, it's theirs—no strings attached. But if they choose the second gift, they'll need to pay five cents to get it. They can get the money from other kids in the room or out of their own pockets—it doesn't matter.

Next, flip a coin, and let the winner pick which gift she wants. She'll most likely choose the five-cent gift (the second one). But it won't diminish the point of this object lesson if she doesn't.

After both volunteers have returned to their seats with their spoils, ask, **Which was the better gift?** I have no way of predicting how your kids will respond to this question because, well, they're junior highers, and they're about as predictable as weather in Chicago. They might have a great discussion with differing opinions—some rare sharp kid might even guess the point of your object lesson. Or, just as likely, they'll all agree with whatever the first person says, which will probably be, "The second one!"

Either way, ask, **Was the second item really a gift?** Again, who knows what they'll say. Modify these next few sentences based on their collective response, but say something like this, **No, the [second item] wasn't really a gift at all because I made [name of volunteer] pay me for it. The price wasn't high, but she still had to pay for it—so it wasn't really a gift. What makes something a gift?** [It has to be free. It's also only a gift if the giver doesn't expect to get it back—otherwise it's a loan.]

Now read Luke 2:1-20 from *The Message*. It's printed out for you on page 17. Read it through while you're preparing for your group so you can read it smoothly and with clarity and emphasis.

After you've read this moving passage, say, **God tells us in Ephesians 2:8 that our salvation is a gift from him—we didn't do anything to earn it, we can't buy it, and he won't take it back. But the Bible shows us that God is more than a giftgiver—he's actually a gift himself.**

Ask:
• **How is God a gift in the passage I just read to you?** [He wrapped himself up and became a little baby, just for us.]
• **What difference does it make that he gave himself as a gift?** [All the difference in the world! He couldn't give us the gift of salvation apart from giving us himself.]
• **What's the difference between giving a gift (stuff) and giving yourself as a gift?** [Giving yourself as a gift is riskier. If someone rejects the gift, they've rejected you. And if someone accepts the gift, then you've really got to start giving!]

Self-portrait

Mini-Dramas

Before you jump into this exercise, ask these questions:

• **How can you, as a young teen, be a gift to someone?** (I don't mean how can you *give* a gift, but how can you *be* a gift.) [Junior highers, just like the rest of us, can be gifts by encouraging, building up, serving, and loving others.]

• **When was the last time someone was a gift to you? How was he a gift?**
• **When was the last time you were a gift to someone? How were you a gift?**

Turn your whole room into a giant meter. Point to one wall and designate it the *extremely cool gift* wall. Point to the opposite wall and designate it the *totally lame gift* wall. Now read this list of ways teens can *be* gifts, and have your students move to one wall or the other, or somewhere in-between, to register their feelings about how good a gift your statement is.

• **Write an encouraging letter to someone who's not your best friend**
• **Sit with a lonely kid at lunch**
• **Tell some kid you'll be nice to her if she pays you**
• **Do one of your brother's or sister's chores without expecting anything in return**

Since this is probably the first lesson you're teaching in this book (unless you're a total renegade who likes to teach the book backward!), it's important that you take a few minutes here to explain the major idea behind this book (it's the same idea behind *Wild Truth Journal—Pictures of God*): God is so great and powerful and amazing—way beyond our understanding—that we can't totally know or understand him. Through the Bible he gave us a bunch of pictures of himself to help us understand him. And since the Bible says we are created in God's image, then these traits must also be in us. That doesn't mean we are little gods! It just means we should be able to put into practice the good and wonderful traits of God. Just like I inherited my dad's nose and my mom's taste for salty foods, so should these pictures of God be evident in me, since I'm a child of God! Get it? Make sure your kids do.

- **Tell your mom and dad you love them**
- **Clean your room, then tell your mom about it 16 times**
- **Make cookies for a family friend**
- **Visit an elderly neighbor**
- **Listen to a friend's problems while huffing, looking at your watch, and making it obvious that you'd rather be anywhere else**
- **Thank your pastor for all his hard work**
- **Volunteer for a day at a local charity or community center**

Now divide your group into teams of about five each. If your whole group is five kids, then, duh, you'll have approximately *one* group. If your group is huge, you could make the teams a little larger. In other words: *modify this stuff to make it work for your group!*

Ask each group to come up with a mini-drama showing one student being a gift to another. Each drama should have at least three people in it: two actors and a narrator. The narrator should tell everyone who the characters are and, at the end, how the student was a gift.

Give the groups about five minutes to put their dramas together. If you have enough adult leaders, it would be great to have one sit in each group. Otherwise, you should roam around the room to make sure the groups are staying on task (What? A group of junior highers getting off task? Never!).

Then (um, isn't this obvious?) have the groups perform their masterpieces.

Hey! I'm a Gift!

Distribute copies of **Hey, I'm a Gift!** (page 18) and pens or pencils to your students. Then sit back and watch the destruction begin. No, really, read through the sheet with them, then read your own plan of action as an example (yup, model

this stuff for 'em!). Give them a few minutes to write on their own papers.

When it seems like they've done all they're going to do, ask a few kids to share their action plans. Tell them you'll ask them about this next week. (Don't forget!)

OPTIONAL CRAFT
Make a Gift

Have kids make a gift for someone. It could be a card, a drawing, or a weird piece of modern art! But whatever it is, it should be designed to encourage the receiver.

Close in prayer. First, have kids finish this sentence in prayer: **God, thanks for the gift you've given me of ...** Then ask God for courage and wisdom to be great gifts to other people this week and to follow through on our gift action plans.

HANDY REVIEW OPTION
Weekly Wall Art

If you're going to teach most or all of the lessons in this book, it would be cool to make a sign for your room that says GOD IS LIKE ... and add a symbol each week to represent the picture you discussed. You can make a simple sketch of your own or enlarge and reproduce the sketch on the first page of ach chapter. For this week you could have a large graphic of a wrapped present. This would help the kids remember the series, as well as get a bigger picture of who God is and what he's like.

Amazing Grace Soul Detergent

Characters:
  Announcer
  Housewife

The stage is set with a large bowl resting on a table. Under the table is a box about the size and shape of a powder soap box, with a fake label stuck on it that says AMAZING GRACE SOUL DETERGENT. *The Housewife is standing at the bowl and scrubbing at a black T-shirt, while looking tired and bored. A white T-shirt is hidden in the bowl. The announcer comes up beside her. This drama is best if both characters overact, using exaggerated TV voices.*

ANNOUNCER: And what have we here? A poor old woman doing her laundry.

HOUSEWIFE: Who are you calling old?

ANNOUNCER: May I ask what you're washing today, madam?

HOUSEWIFE: Oh, just my soul.

ANNOUNCER: Ah, one of those wash-day nightmares.

HOUSEWIFE: Tell me about it. I wash and I scrub and I just can't seem to get the dirt out.

ANNOUNCER: It's a common dilemma seen every day in households around the world.

HOUSEWIFE: I mean, this soul is supposed to be clean. Just look at it. **(holds up black T-shirt)**

ANNOUNCER: Well, have you tried Grace?

HOUSEWIFE: Grace? What's that?

ANNOUNCER: (whips out brightly colored box of Grace from under the table) Grace is the new total soul-stain solution. Created in the laboratories of God to whisk away those stubborn stains of sin from your soul and leave it bright, pure, and morning-fresh.

HOUSEWIFE: I don't see how it can remove these stains. I've been washing this soul all my life, and it just seems to get darker and darker.

ANNOUNCER: But ordinary scrubbing and cleaning can't shift the dirt of sin. In fact, nothing you do can remove the grime and filth that you've accumulated on your soul. Independent laboratory tests prove that only Grace will remove the stain of sin—there's simply nothing you can do to remove it yourself. Grace has special active ingredients created by God and distributed through Jesus that will clean out those stains forever!

HOUSEWIFE: Hmm. I'm not sure...

ANNOUNCER: Well, let's put it to the test. Would you like to try some Grace?

HOUSEWIFE: Well... all right, why not?

Announcer sprinkles powder from the box into the bowl, then swirls it around with his finger. Housewife stares into the bowl in disbelief.

ANNOUNCER: Well, what do you think?

HOUSEWIFE: I can't believe it! *(pulls white T-shirt out of the basin)* It was so quick!

ANNOUNCER: That's right. No soaking. No scrubbing. Just instant results.

HOUSEWIFE: And it's so clean! There's not even a shadow of the old stain. It's like brand new.

ANNOUNCER: Yes, Grace makes your soul look, feel, and smell as if sin had never entered the world. Would you like to know where you can get new Grace?

HOUSEWIFE: Ooh, yes please. *(pauses)* But isn't it terribly expensive?

ANNOUNCER: That's what our competitors would have you believe. But as a matter of fact, Grace is totally free!

HOUSEWIFE: Free?

ANNOUNCER: Yes, free! All you have

to do is contact God, through Jesus, and simply ask for it. In no time at all you'll receive a lifetime supply of Grace—all absolutely free!

HOUSEWIFE: How can God make such a wonderful offer?

ANNOUNCER: Because God has unlimited supplies of Grace! And all he wants is to see the souls of this world as clean and bright as they should be.

HOUSEWIFE: It all sounds too wonderful.

ANNOUNCER: It *is* an amazing offer. Hurry and contact Jesus for your free supply of Grace today.

HOUSEWIFE: I'll do it right away.

ANNOUNCER: Well folks, you've heard the good news. You've seen the results. Why not try Grace for yourself and experience this perfect cleanliness in *your* soul? Any final words, madam?

HOUSEWIFE: *(clutching white T-shirt tightly and smiling)* My soul could never have been clean without Grace. Thank you God, and thank you Jesus.

ANNOUNCER: Another satisfied customer of Grace, bought to you by God and distributed by Jesus. God—first in cleanliness, strength, and power for a brighter tomorrow. Thank you and good day.

Lights dim and curtain falls.

End

The Birth of Jesus

About that time Caesar Augustus ordered a census to be taken throughout the Empire. This was the first census when Quirinius was governor of Syria. Everyone had to travel to his own ancestral hometown to be accounted for. So Joseph went from the Galilean town of Nazareth up to Bethlehem in Judah, David's town, for the census. As a descendant of David, he had to go there. He went with Mary, his fiancée, who was pregnant.

While they were there, the time came for her to give birth. She gave birth to a son, her first-born. She wrapped him in a blanket and laid him in a manger, because there was no room for them in the hostel.

An Event for Everyone

There were sheepherders camping in the neighborhood. They had set watches over their sheep. Suddenly, God's angel stood among them and God's glory blazed around them. They were terrified. The angel said, "Don't be afraid. I'm here to announce a great and joyful event that is meant for everybody, worldwide: A Savior who is Messiah and Master. This is what you're to look for: a baby wrapped in a blanket and lying in a manger."

At once the angel was joined by a huge angelic choir singing God's praises:

"Glory to God in the heavenly heights,
Peace to all men and women on earth who please him."

As the angel choir withdrew into heaven, the sheepherders talked it all over. "Let's get over to Bethlehem as fast as we can and see for ourselves what God has revealed to us." They left, running, and found Mary and Joseph, and the baby lying in the manger. Seeing was believing. They told everyone they met what the angels had said about this child. All who heard the sheepherders were impressed.

Mary kept all these things to herself, holding them dear, deep within herself. The sheepherders returned and let loose, glorifying and praising God for everything they had heard and seen. It turned out exactly the way they'd been told.

—Luke 2:1-20 (*The Message*)

Hey, I'm a Gift!

My name is:
- ❑ Herman
- ❑ Prudence
- ❑ other: _____

I'm going to be a gift to someone this week by:
- ❑ loving them
- ❑ encouraging them
- ❑ serving them
- ❑ reaching out to them
- ❑ listening to them
- ❑ other: _____

The person I'm gonna be a gift to is:
- ❑ Herman
- ❑ Prudence
- ❑ other:_____

And (drum roll, please) my big plan of action for doing this is—

18

God is like WATER

O God, you are my God, earnestly I seek you; my soul thirsts for you, my body longs for you, in a dry and weary land where there is no water. **Psalm 63:1**

Students will—
- Understand why God is like water
- Understand how they can be like water by refreshing, quenching, and reviving other people
- Choose a water plan

Picture Prep

Water Games

Start your time with a little water carnival. Most of these games won't require kids to get totally drenched, so they'd still be appropriate for Sunday school, as well as another youth group time. But make sure you're careful about kids' clothing. And make sure you have a bunch of towels on hand! You could make this whole series of games a competition between the guys and the girls or between grades.

You'll need—
- an ice chest full of water with six lemons in it
- a large pan full of water and ice with grapes in it
- four baby bottles full of water
- a Super Soaker filled with water (lots of kids have one of these—you could borrow it instead of buying it)
- a trash bag

Lemon Bobbing
Instead of bobbing for apples, try lemons. Fill an ice chest with water and have contestants (with their hands behind their backs) try to grab the lemons with their teeth. Give a hundred points for every lemon snatched within 15 seconds. Play three rounds so each team has an opportunity to get three lemons.

Toe Grape-Grabbing
Fill a large pan or bowl with water (the colder the better) and lots of ice. Crushed ice is best but anything will work. Put grapes underneath and in the ice. Have contestants use their toes to try to grab grapes. Play a few rounds and give them 50 points for each grape they grab within 15 seconds (they can grab more than one per round). If you're a little sick and twisted (you work with junior highers—isn't this obvious?), consider giving bonus points for kids who will eat the grapes.

Water Bottle
Get four baby bottles (they're really cheap if you buy the—well, the cheap ones!) and fill them with water. Take a pin or a knife and make the hole in the end of the nipple a bit larger (this game will take *forever* otherwise!). Have two contestants from each team race to guzzle the water. Give 200 points for first place, 100 points for second place, and 50 points for third.

Super Soaker Drink
Fill a Super Soaker with water. In case you've been living in a space station for the last decade, a Super Soaker is a high-powered squirt gun that shoots water a long way. Rip a head-hole in the end of a trash bag and have each contestant (one at a time, one from each team) place it over her

head to keep her *somewhat* dry. Then stand at a distance and squirt right at her mouth. Have a neutral judge decide which contestant was better at drinking from the Super Soaker. By the way, it's inevitable that you'll spray a little water on this one. The floor will get a bit wet. The Ralph W. Peterson Memorial Wallpaper might get a drop of water on it. So be warned!

OPTIONAL GAME
Water Fight!

If your group isn't meeting on Sunday morning in pretty clothes, and if the weather's warm enough, consider having an all-out water war. Don't tell the kids what you have planned. Tell them it's a water balloon tossing game. Get them all outside, and pull out a trash can full of pre-made water balloons. (Here's a tip: put water in the trash can so the balloons don't rub against each other and break.) Have kids pair up and stand facing each other. Each time they toss the balloon, have them move one step farther apart.

Okay, that's the boring part. But you, and your volunteers, know the real plan! Have a bunch of small buckets of water and a hose with a spray nozzle ready. Once the kids are concentrating on their little tossing activity—nail 'em! Just go crazy and start a massive water war free-for-all. Your kids will be caught off guard that you would do something so uncontrolled—something you'd usually scold them for. You'll create a fun group memory and a bunch of soggy kids!

You'll need—
• water balloons
• hoses
• buckets
• a water source

Action shot

Multiple-Choice Melodrama

Ask for two volunteers, a guy and a girl, to play parts in a little melodrama. Explain that they don't have to read any parts— they just have to act out the action as you read it. And if there are any spoken parts, you'll say

them, and they just have to repeat them.

Then tell the whole group they're going to see the same story three times. Each time it will be a little bit different. Their job is to decide which of the stories is the closest to the actual Bible story.

Now read the three stories on page 23 and have the actors ham it up. Each time there's a spoken part, read the line, then pause for the actor to repeat it.

After you read and act out all three versions, have the kids vote for the one they think is closest to the real thing. The correct answer is the third one—and this will be obvious to all but those kids who weren't paying attention. The only kids who'll vote for another

You'll need—
• one copy of *Multiple Choice Melodrama* (page 23)

answer are those seventh grade boys who think, *Ooh, it'll be really, really funny if I vote for the wrong answer! Ha! I'm so funny!* But it doesn't matter if they all get it right—that will just make them feel good.

Have everyone turn in their Bibles to John 4

and follow along while you read the real story from verses 4-14. Realize this is a tough mental leap for most of your kids—to perceive how Jesus is "living water that quenches our souls." So you might have to unpack the idea for them a bit by talking, just like Jesus did, about thirst. But first, ask if anyone can explain how God is like water, according to this passage. If they can't come up with a reasonable explanation (which is likely), read this list of things water does, and ask kids to stand up for those things that God also does. Each time kids are standing, ask one of them to explain what they mean.

- **rehydrates (makes dry things moist)**
- **quenches thirst**
- **flushes bad stuff out of our bodies**
- **dissolves things**
- **cleans**
- **knows how to spell *chrysanthemum***
- **cools**
- **refreshes**

Now probably half of your kids (the older ones) are starting to understand this abstract concept, but you'll probably need to go one step further for the other kids.

Explain by saying, **It's like this. Our souls, the deepest spiritual part of who we are, get thirsty. Not for real water, but for something that will make us come alive. People try to quench this thirst with wild living and partying, with money, with adrenaline rushes; but none of those things will take away the thirst in your soul—Jesus will. That's why he's called *living water* because he's alive and he satisfies all our needs.**

normal for young teens, these writing utensils will soon become weapons of destruction. Ah, well.

Ask the groups to read through these short descriptions of teens who were like water and rank them in order. Tell them they have to work as a team to decide which teen is most water-like (that would be number eight) all the way down to the one who's least water-like (that would be number one). Now give the groups about five minutes to work. Don't forget to circulate around the room to make sure they understand what they're supposed to be doing. By the way, if they give the story about Rick dumping water on his brother's head a high rating, that will be a good clue they still don't understand this water picture!

After several minutes, or after all your kids

You'll need—
- copies of **Water Kidz** (page 24)
- pens or pencils

seem to be talking about movies and music instead of this assignment, pull them back together and debrief. Ask them who they rated high, who they rated low, and why for both. Then ask your students to look over the stories again. Ask them to rate the stories on their own sheets, again from eight to one, to reflect which of these situations would be most difficult for them to do (eight is easiest to do; one is most difficult to do).

Then, after a few more minutes, debrief this as well, asking the students what they put at the top and bottom and why.

Water Rating

Move students into groups of about three each. Pass out (that means distribute, not fall to the floor!) copies of **Water Kidz** (page 24) and writing utensils to your students. If they're anywhere within 10 degrees of

Takin' it Home

Finally, have them look at their wildpage one more time. This time ask them to choose one of those ideas to try this week. Tell them that if they're willing to try one of them, they should cross out the character's name and write their own above it, then circle that whole idea. Also tell them that they can make up a new plan and write it on the back of the sheet if they want. Again, have a few students share their answers.

Then close in prayer, asking God for courage to follow through on these water-like behaviors and thanking him for being living water in our lives.

HANDY REVIEW OPTION
Weekly Wall Art

If you're using the signs idea described in Lesson 1, add a graphic of some water. Just color a large piece of paper or posterboard blue, then scallop one edge to look like waves.

Multiple-Choice Melodrama

Version 1

One day Jesus was walking along a road, just whistling a happy tune, when he realized he was thirsty.

"Hey…," he said *(pause)*, "I'm thirsty!" *(pause)*

There was a lady over on the other side of the road selling water. She kept yelling, "Water! Get yer ice-cold water here!" *(pause)*

Jesus walked over to the lady and asked, "Can I have some water?" *(pause)*

She handed him a cup, and he drank and sighed a big ol' sigh of relief. Then he said, "Thanks!" *(pause)*, and left. The lady went on yelling about her water. *(pause)*

Version 2

One day Jesus was riding down a road on a horse. The horse was a little uncontrollable and kept veering off the road into the kids sitting in chairs nearby.

Jesus said, "Whoa, horsy!" *(pause)* and the horse moved back onto the road.

Alongside the road there was a well. A woman was standing by it and pulling up a bucket of water. She was singing a song about water that sounded like she was just making it up. *(pause)* In fact, she sang it even louder. *(pause)* Then she started doing a little dance to the tune of the song. *(pause)*

Jesus watched all this, rubbed his chin, and said, "Hmm." *(pause)* He hopped down off his horse, walked over to the lady, and said, "Excuse me." *(pause)*

Startled, she whirled around and shrieked.

Jesus said, "Sorry," *(pause)* "I didn't mean to startle you." *(pause)* "But I was wondering" *(pause)* "if you could refresh me with some of your water." *(pause)*

The lady didn't understand that he was thirsty, so she said, "Sure," *(pause)* and tossed a cup of water in his face.

Version 3

Jesus was sitting by a well. He was tired from a long walk and was starting to fall asleep. Then this woman showed up and started pulling water out of the well with a bucket.

Jesus asked her, "Can I have some of your water?" *(pause)*

She said, "Why me?" *(pause)*

Jesus answered, "If you knew who I was, you'd ask me for living water." *(pause)*

She said, "I don't have a clue what you're talking about." *(pause)*

Jesus explained, "I can quench the thirst in your soul." *(pause)*

And everyone in the room said, "Oh, I get it." *(pause—make sure all the kids in the room say this line together.)*

Water Kidz

Rank these students from eight (most water-like) down to one (least water-like).

____ Karen's friend treated her like a jerk in front of a bunch of other kids. Karen thought of this totally cool way to get revenge, but she knew the tension between her and her friend would just get worse if she did this. So instead of getting even with her friend, Karen forgave her and extinguished a fiery situation.

____ Carly noticed a girl in her gym class that she'd never seen before. And then she noticed her again at lunch. The girl may have always been at Carly's school, but Carly had never noticed her before. And apparently no one else had either because the girl was by herself. Carly decided to sit with her at lunch to quench the girl's need to know someone cares about her.

____ Rick can't stand it. His brother always gets his own way, and Rick never does. So today he did something to make himself feel better about it. He rigged up a bucket of water over his brother's bedroom door. When his brother opened the door, the water came splashing down on his brother's head. It was totally cool.

____ Nikki's friend, Jenna, has started going to some pretty wild parties. The kids at the parties are popular, and Jenna loves to think she's part of their group. Nikki knew it was only going to cause trouble for Jenna, that pretty soon she'd probably start drinking alcohol all the time, and who knows what else would follow. So Nikki took a chance that Jenna would hurt her feelings and told her, "Jenna, I really care about you, but I'm afraid that you're headed for trouble. I think you're going to get involved in stuff that will hurt you." By doing this, Nikki was part of a cleaning process in Jenna's life.

____ There are a bunch of crabby old people in Jason's church; but Jason has decided he's going to be nice to them and treat them with respect. His actions are refreshing.

____ Chad didn't want to obey his parents. He didn't feel like obeying his parents. So when he chose to obey them anyway, they were totally surprised. It refreshed all of them like a fun waterfight.

____ Christiana did something pretty hard today. She chose to make it a rehydration day. All day long she served people without ever expecting anything in return. In doing so, she was rehydrating their dry lives. (If you don't know what *rehydrate* means, ask your leader.)

____ Kass was a dissolver today! He smiled and was friendly to the weird old man down the street whom no one ever talks to. By doing this, Kass softened up the old guy's hard heart.

24

God is like a RESCUE WORKER

For he has rescued us from the dominion of darkness and brought us into the kingdom of the Son he loves.   Colossians 1:13

Students will—

- Understand why God is like a rescue worker
- Understand how they can be like a rescue worker to others when they focus on other peoples' needs instead of their own
- List some people they might be able to help

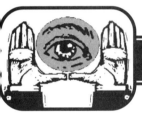

Picture Prep

Rescue!

Distribute copies of **Rescue!** (page 29) and pens or pencils (or crayons or eyeliner) to each student. Explain that when you say, "Go!" they're to complete the activities on this sheet and get people to initial the items to prove they did them. They can do them in any order they want, but they can't get the same person's initials more than once. If your

You'll need—
- copies of **Rescue!** (page 29)
- pens or pencils
- (optional) small candy bars or some other prize for first and second place

group is large enough (20 or more), add the rule that they can't do any of the activities with the same people—they have to find new people for each one.

Read the activities out

loud to make sure everyone understands them. Then shout "Go!" Mill around to make sure kids aren't cheating. Then, when the first two kids bring you their completed sheets, declare the game over and have everyone return to their seats. If you have small prizes, award them to the first and second place winners.

Make a transition by asking, **Have you ever been rescued from something?** (Have kids share if they have stories. If you don't get enough responses, rephrase the question to, "Have you ever seen someone be rescued?" and have them share stories). Then say something like, **In real life we need rescue workers when we get into a physical problem that we can't get out of on our own. God's like a rescue worker too, and he rescues us from stuff we'd never get out of on our own.**

OPTIONAL VIDEO
Rescue Scene

If you use this idea, use it after the game and before the transition discussion.

Help kids visualize a rescue by showing one (or two). Use a clip from a movie that shows a rescue scene, and just show that little piece of the video. Here are some ideas.

You'll need—
- a rescue scene from a movie
- TV
- VCR

- Any number of scenes from the movie *Backdraft*.
- The scene from Robert DiNiro's movie *Ronin*, following a long car chase where two people are pulled from an overturned car just before it explodes.
- The scene from Bruce Willis' movie *Mercury Rising*, where he saves a child from an oncoming train.
- The scene from Sandra Bullock's movie *While You Were Sleeping*, where she rolls a man off the train tracks just before the train arrives.

My Rescue Words

Have students turn in their Bibles to Colossians 1:13 and ask for a volunteer to read it. Then ask them to use the blank back side of the **Rescue!** wildpage to rewrite that verse in their own words. Give them about a minute to do this. Then have a few kids share their translations.

Next ask, **How, exactly, does God do this rescuing?** Ask them to write an answer on their sheets before getting a few responses.

Finally, ask them to write their own rescue story—how God rescued them—on their sheets. Again, give them time to work individually before asking for a few to share.

Be aware here that some kids might not have rescue stories because they've never been rescued. Use this as an opportunity, if this situation becomes clear, to talk to kids about the rescue God offers us—rescue from hell, yes, but also rescue from a meaningless, empty life here on earth.

You'll probably also have some kids who do have a relationship with God but have no idea when they were rescued or what they were rescued from. Talk this through with them. Ask them

You'll need—
- the blank back side of the wildpage just completed
- pens or pencils
- Bibles

Sixth Sense

Many school districts have moved to a middle school model, grouping sixth through eighth grades together—thereby forcing churches to rethink the positioning of their sixth graders.

At least three good options make effective ministry possible to these youngest of teens:

- You can lobby for a fifth and sixth grade preteen ministry. Run it like a youth ministry, as opposed to a children's Sunday school program, making it age appropriate and requiring high parental involvement.
- You can request that sixth-graders be incorporated into your junior ministry—but still provide separate settings for most activities.
- If your sixth-graders are already combined with seventh- and eighth-graders, you can use grade specific small groups to tackle sensitive subjects in age-appropriate ways.

From *Help! I'm a Junior High Youth Worker!* by Mark Oestreicher (Youth Specialties).

to think about how their life would be different if they didn't know God. Explain that God never promises us a perfect life (happiness, wealth, complete health), but he does promise to rescue us from sin and separation from him, which is the most important rescue of all!

OPTIONAL VIDEO
Live the Life Rescue Story

Youth Specialties, in conjunction with Youth for Christ, produced a fantastic resource called *Live the Life*, based on the DC/LA '97 mega-event. It's a video curriculum designed to help students learn how to share their faith—and it's awesome! The description of the gospel throughout the video series is referred to as "God's Rescue Story." It visualizes this with a fun, edgy, animated sequence that pops up multiple times throughout the curriculum. Show this bit to your kids (and even the talking head material surrounding its first description) as a way of clarifying this picture of God.

You'll need—
- *Live the Life* video curriculum
- TV
- VCR

OPTIONAL DRAMA
The Lemon

Use the drama on pages 30-31 to illustrate, from a different perspective, the idea of God rescuing us. This short drama will work best if the actors rehearse it ahead of time, but you could also pull it off with good readers who read the parts spontaneously.

After the drama, ask this series of questions—

You'll need—
- two copies of **The Lemon** (pages 30-31)
- two semi-prepared actors
- two empty chairs
- a little scrap of paper

- **Who's the seller?** *[We are]*
- **What does the car represent?** *[Our rotten, sinful lives!]*
- **Who was the buyer?** *[God]*
- **Why didn't anything work on the car?** *[There's nothing worth saving about you and me. God doesn't save us because we're good or wonderful. He saves us because he loves us! That's it.]*
- **What did God have to pay to rescue us?** *[Jesus' life]*

Say something like, **Okay, here's the deal. God *is* a rescuer because he saves us from sin and hell. But we can be *like* rescue workers too.**

Self-portrait

Talk Show

Before your group meets, ask three kids to help you with this activity. Their part is very simple. You're going to stage a fake talk show, Oprah-style! These three volunteers will be the guests. Give each of them a copy of the **Talk Show!** script on page 32 and assign their parts. You

You'll need—
- four copies of **Talk Show!** (page 32)
- four chairs
- (optional) a sign that says APPLAUSE

play the part of the host.

When it's time to begin, tell the kids you've just transformed your youth group room into a TV studio, and they get to be the live studio audience for the first edition of "_____"! (Name the show after yourself, make a big deal about how cool the name is.) It would be even more fun (is it possible?) if you had a student or adult volunteer come to the front and hold a sign that says APPLAUSE, signaling the audience when they should whoop it up!

After you've explained the setup, say, **We roll tape in, five, four, three, two...,** and then launch into your opening while looking at an imaginary TV camera. Introduce your three guests and have them take a seat up front. The fourth chair is for you when you're not roaming the audience.

Say something like, **Our topic today is "I can be a rescue worker." Our three guests have come to get advice. Each of them will share their stories, and then we'll ask our wonderful studio audience for advice on how these teens can be rescue workers in their situations. Okay?** You get the idea—ham it up. Be obnoxious. Be Jerry Springer!

Have the first guest read (or describe without the script, if she's able) her script to describe her situation. Then jump into talk show-host mode and get the studio audience to give her ideas on how she can be a rescue worker. Ask follow-up questions to those who offer suggestions.

After you've exhausted ideas for the first guest, move on to the second and then the third. When you've finished getting ideas for all three guests' stories, close the show with a flourish and invite everyone back next week. Then transform your studio back into your youth group room!

Say something like, **Okay, we've seen a few examples of junior highers who wanted to be rescue workers. But here's the big trick—you can never be a rescue worker until you look for other peoples' needs. And you can't see *their* needs if you're always focusing on your own needs.**

Need Spotting

Pass out copies of **Need Spotting** (page 33) to each of your students. They should still have pens or pencils from your opening exercise, although if they're pencils, most of the boys have broken them into toothpicks by now; and if they were pens (note I said "were"), some McGyver kid has figured out how to dismantle it and make a miniature cannon. Don't you love working with young teens?

Back to need spotting. Ask your students to work individually for a few minutes and try to think of needs that their friends and family might have. Walk around and see if they understand this.

Then after a few minutes, have them take a crack at the bottom half of the sheet, which asks them to create a rescue plan for one of the people they listed on the top half of the page. Help them understand that we

can offer rescue and try to help people; but if they don't want help, we can't force it on them.

Have a few kids share their ideas after they've finished.

Then close your group in prayer.

HANDY REVIEW OPTION
Weekly Wall Art

If you're using the signs idea described at the end of Lesson 1, add a big graphic of a hard hat or fireman's hat to your wall.

Rescue!

Complete these items in any order you choose, and get someone's initials to prove you did them. However, you have to get a *different* person's initials on each one.

Kitten in the Tree
Stand on a chair and meow like a cat caught in a tree. Have a rescue worker lift you off the chair, then have that person initial here: _____

Heart Attack in the Woods
Get three other people and pretend you're on a hike in the woods by walking all the way around the room in single file. Upon circling the room, the person with the shortest hair suddenly has a heart attack, and the other three have to carry him to safety (which happens to be the front of the room). Have two of the hikers initial here: _____ _____

Jaws of Life
Get two other people and arrange chairs like you're in a car—two in the front seat and one in the back. Then pretend the car crashes (all the chairs fall over!). The person in the back seat is trapped! Shout, "Here come the jaws of life!" and pull the chairs off the trapped person. After all three of you hug each other and pretend to cry tears of joy, have one of them initial here: _____

Castaways
You and another person stand on chairs in the corner—that's your uncharted desert island. After your ship sank, you've been living there for five years (mess up your hair a little!). Get the attention of someone on the far side of the room (they can't be right next to you), by yelling, "Help! We're stranded!" When that person comes over to you, consider yourself rescued. Have one of the other people initial here: _____

Bad Fall
Lie down on the floor and start yelling, "I've fallen, and I can't get up!" As soon as you find someone willing to help you up, have them initial here: _____ (Then do the same for them!)

Fire!
Get three other people. Two of you pretend you're in a burning house. Yell, "Fire!" ten times. Once you've completed this, the other two people can be the firemen. They should pretend they're spraying the fire while yelling, "We'll rescue you!" five times. Once this is all done, have two of those people initial here: _____ _____

The Lemon

Characters
Owner
Buyer

The car owner and the car buyer are on stage. In front of them is a car, represented by two chairs standing side-by-side to look like a front seat. The owner needs a little scrap of paper in his pocket to show the price to the buyer.

BUYER: Hello. I'm here about the car.

OWNER: Oh, yeah, thanks for coming. It's just over here.

BUYER: *(seeing car)* Oh…

OWNER: Yeah, it's not much to look at, I admit. Still… um… it was a classic year.

BUYER: *(running hand along a fender)* It's a bit rusty.

OWNER: Well, you can cut that out.

BUYER: I suppose so. *(tries to open the door, making a great show of effort, and eventually it opens with a very loud squeal)* These hinges could use some oil, too.

OWNER: Couldn't we all? Ha! Ha! Ha!

BUYER: *(sits on the seat and tries to get comfortable)* What happened to this seat? Were you storing knives in here? This upholstery is trashed!

OWNER: Yeah… they don't make vinyl like they used to.

BUYER: *(places hands experimentally on steering wheel and turns it a little; it comes off in his hands)* Uh, the steering wheel just came off in my hands!

OWNER: I think it's meant to do that.

BUYER: Sure. How about the radio? *(turns on radio, pretends to push buttons)* What's wrong with this radio? Every station is the same.

OWNER: I dunno. It's always done that. It's the darndest thing. The volume's stuck too.

BUYER: *(turns radio off in disgust and gets out, after another fight with the door; he walks around and attempts to open the trunk, and has the same trouble opening it as he did with the door. Eventually it opens and the Buyer reels back from an awful smell)* Good grief, what is that smell? What have you been putting in here?

OWNER: Oh, you know how it is. You find something by the side of the road, it looks kinda neat, and you throw it in the trunk. After a while you sorta forget what you've put in there. *(peers into the trunk and makes a face at the smell)* I guess I should have been more careful.

BUYER: *(struggles to close the trunk then continues to walk around car. Pats rear fender to test for strength)* Oh great, the fender fell off.

OWNER: That'll just bolt right back on.

BUYER: *(looks unconvinced and kicks the front tire)* I kick it, it goes flat. I think the tires could use some work too.

OWNER: Nothing a little tender loving care can't fix.

BUYER: Hmm. *(wanders around to the front of the car and, with the usual struggle, manages to open the hood. Looks inside)*

OWNER: What do you think?

BUYER: There's a hamster in a little plastic wheel hooked up to the drive train.

OWNER: Yeah... so it's not the original engine. He's one strong little hamster, that fella.

BUYER: This is, without a doubt, the worst car I have ever seen in my life. How much are you asking for this?

OWNER: *(hands scrap of paper to Buyer. Buyer staggers in shock)*

BUYER: What! I could buy a new car for that!

OWNER: But this is a classic. A collector's item.

BUYER: It's a trashy piece of junk! I'd have a more reliable transportation if I hooked that hamster up to a skateboard!

OWNER: Yeah, but would it keep out the rain?

BUYER: Would that roof?

OWNER: Well, no, but....

BUYER: This is the most appalling, ugly, badly maintained vehicle I have ever seen. Tell me, what are you going to do with it if I don't buy it?

OWNER: I guess I'll have to sell it for scrap.

BUYER: *(pause)* You mean it will be destroyed?

OWNER: I'm afraid so. There's nothing else for it.

BUYER: No one else is willing to restore it?

OWNER: No one else can be bothered.

BUYER: Then... I'll take it.

OWNER: What?

BUYER: I'll take it. I'll pay your price for it.

OWNER: You'd pay this *(points at paper)* for that *(points at car)*?

BUYER: You said so yourself—this car is doomed. If I don't buy it, nobody else will.

OWNER: Is it worth it?

BUYER: It has to be. Here's a check. I'll be coming again. I'll pick it up then. *(looks at car, sighs, then exits)*

OWNER: *(stands in disbelief for a couple seconds, then jumps up in the air and shouts)* Yeah!

Lights dim and curtain falls.

End

Talk Show!

Guest 1

Annalisa

Hi, I'm Annalisa. Here's my situation. I have this friend named Brooke who's really depressed. She used to be fun, but now she's down all the time. I've tried to reach out to her, but I'm not sure what to do or say. How can I be a rescue worker for Brooke?

Guest 2

Jason

Hey, it's great to be on the _____ show. I never thought I could be a guest! Anyhow, my name's Jason, and I can tell my dad's stressed out right now. He brings work home every night, and it doesn't seem like he's getting any sleep. He's cranky and doesn't have any time for fun. How can I be a rescue worker for my dad?

Guest 3

Emily

Hi everyone, I'm Emily. I hope you can help me with my rescue problem. It's about Curt, this kid I know from school. Curt's always talking big and showing off. I can tell he's trying to prove he's a big man, but he's really just insecure. Nobody talks to him, and everyone ignores him when he's in his tough-guy mode. I don't know him very well, and I *really* don't want him to think I like him as a boyfriend or anything. How can I be a rescue worker for Curt?

WILDPAGE

Need Spotting

Before you write anything, think for a minute. Try to think of three or four friends, family members, or just people you know who have some kind of need right now. Maybe they're lonely. Maybe they're too busy. Or it could be a need for Jesus, a need for attention, a need for help with a project or school work, or lots of other needs. After thinking for a minute, write down some names and possible needs.

name	possible needs

Now choose one of those people, and put a star next to his or her name. Then in the space below, write down three ideas for how you might try to meet that need—how you might offer rescue. After you've written all three ideas, pray about it and choose one you'll try this week.

1.

2.

3.

33

God is like a ROCK

From the ends of the earth I call to you, I call as my heart grows faint; lead me to the rock that is higher than I. Psalm 61:2

Students will—

- Understand why God is like a rock
- Understand how they can be like a rock by growing in integrity and being trustworthy
- Take steps to correct a time when they were untrustworthy

Picture Prep

Rock War

Start your time by making fake rocks and playing a few games with them. First, make the rocks by having kids wad up sheets of newspaper and wrap a few strips of masking tape around the ball. The masking tape will hold it together, but it will also make it more streamlined for throwing. Each student should make about four rocks.

After the rocks are made, your students' hands will probably be a mess from the newspaper ink. You might want to offer Handiwipes to them, or some other method of washing their hands. Otherwise the ink will get all over their clothes, faces, and the room (maybe you'd prefer this!).

Now divide your students into two groups. It's best to do this along natural lines that would semi-evenly split the group: seventh grade versus eighth grade, guys versus girls, or kids with newspaper ink on their faces versus kids with newspaper ink on their clothes. Move the two groups to opposite sides of the room and indicate where the middle is.

Tell them round one of this game calls for them to get as many rocks as possible on the other side of the room. Then start the game. If you play some rowdy music while they're throwing, it adds to the fun. After a couple minutes, stop the game (this is tricky—some over-energetic kid will always think it's okay to keep tossing rocks to the other side!). Take a rough count of the rocks on each side and declare a winner.

Now play round two. For this round their goal is to get as many rocks as possible on their *own* side. Tell them they can't hold onto the rocks—they can only pick them up to throw them. And for this round they're allowed to cross the middle line as much as they want. Then start the game (and the frenetic music, if you have it). Stand back—this could be a free-for-all! After a couple minutes, stop the game and declare a winning side.

After the paramedics leave and the blood is cleaned up, ask these obvious questions—

- **How would this game have been different if we'd played with real rocks?**
- **What would you have done if I'd brought in a bunch of rocks and told you to play that game?**

Then ask kids to give you as many descriptive words for rocks as they can think of. Some possibilities are hard, strong, heavy, steady, unmoving, solid, unchanging, still, and dependable.

You'll need—
- newspaper (about one for every 10 kids)
- masking tape (about one roll for every four kids)
- Handiwipes or some other way to wash hands

OPTIONAL IDEA
Rock Climbing

Yeah, I know this isn't feasible for many people—that's why I made it optional. But if you can get your kids to a place where you're able to do some rock climbing, or even just some boulder scrambling, you'll bring your kids a long way toward understanding the importance of the rock's stability.

You'll need—
- boulders or a rock wall
- rock climbing equiment

TV Commercials

Divide your students into groups of four or five. (Remember, if your group is small—four or five kids total—or really large, customize, customize, customize!) Ask your students to look up and read the following three verses.

You'll need—
- Bibles

- Psalm 18:2
- Psalm 61:2
- Isaiah 26:4

62:12

It would be helpful if you could put these references on an overhead projector or a whiteboard, so they don't have to ask you 47,000 times which passages they're supposed to read.

Instruct the groups to put together a 30-second commercial for God the Rock. Give them about five minutes to work on this. Move around the room to offer help where necessary.

Then have the groups perform their commercials. If you have a bunch of groups and they start running longer than 30 seconds, give them a 10-second warning as to when you'll cut it off (which should probably be about 45 seconds into their time!).

After they finish their performances, have them discuss this question in their groups: **What difference does it make that God is like a rock?** After a minute or so, ask for responses.

Make a transition by saying something like,

When the Bible talks about God being a rock, it's talking about how much we can depend on him. What makes a person dependable? *[You can always believe what they say, you can count on them to do what they say they'll do, they keep their word.]*

Integrity Shuffle

Ask, **What does it mean to have integrity?** *[Most kids won't know the answer to this—and that's okay. But it's great to give kids an opportunity to answer if they think they know. And who knows—some kid might totally surprise you!]*

Use the following illustration to describe integrity.

When you go to a furniture store, some pieces of furniture—the expensive ones—are described as *solid wood.* Many of the other pieces of

You'll need—
- no materials, although having a piece of solid wood and a piece of veneer-covered pressboard would really drive home the illustration

36

furniture *look* like wood and might even have a thin layer of real wood on the outside, called a *veneer*, but they're not solid wood. You could say that a piece of furniture that looks like wood but isn't wood all the way through doesn't have *integrity*. But a piece of furniture that's solid wood does. *Integrity* means you are who you say you are. Your word is good. People can believe you. You aren't hiding things. And you're not pretending to be something or someone you're not.

Ask, **Okay, now who can define integrity for me?** (Get a few answers to see if they understand.)

Explain that you're going to play Integrity Shuffle. You'll say, **"If you've ever done this thing, move two seats to the right,"** or something like that. If the statement is true about you, then you have to move that many seats. If someone is sitting in that seat, sit on top of them. If there are two or three people already stacked up, just join the stack! Tell them that if they get to the end of a row, they should circle around to the other end of the row and continue playing. Now have everyone stand up, then read this list:

- **If you've ever answered a question then changed your mind as soon as the person was gone, move three seats to the right.**
- **If you've ever wimped-out on a friend who really needed your help, move two seats backward.** (If kids don't seem willing to move, encourage them with, "Come on, we've all done this!")
- **If there was at least one time in the last week when you didn't tell the truth, move four seats to the left.**
- **If you've ever cheated on homework or a quiz or a test, move one seat forward.**
- **If you've pretended to be someone you're not, either online or in real life, move five seats to the right.**
- **If you've ever broken a promise, move three seats to the left.**
- **If you've ever made up a lame excuse for not doing something you said you'd do, move three seats backward.**
- **If you act differently around different people, move one seat to the right.**

After everyone returns to their original seats, say something like, **See? We've all lacked integrity at times. We've all been the opposite of a rock at times. But we can be a rock for our friends and family if we grow in integrity and if people can trust us.**

Integrity Worksheet

Distribute copies of **Foam-Core or Solid Wood?** (page 38) and pens or pencils to your students. Give them about five minutes to fill it out. Then have them pull together into groups of two or three and share their answers. Make sure you field ideas from question 4—What can I do?—with the whole group .

For your closing prayer, tell kids you're going to say the first half of a sentence and you want some of them to complete it in prayer. Then lead in prayer with these half-sentences:

> **You'll need—**
> - copies of **Foam-Core or Solid Wood?** (page 38)
> - pens or pencils

- **Lord, help me to be more like a rock by...**
- **God, I know I can have more integrity if I...**
- **Jesus, thank you for...**

HANDY REVIEW OPTION
Weekly Wall Art

If you're using the signs idea described at the end of Lesson 1, add a large graphic of a rock. Just color a large piece of paper or posterboard gray, then cut it into a jagged-edged circle. Make a few black marks on it to give it depth.

Foam-Core or Solid Wood?

1. Which of the following pieces of wood best represents your integrity? (Be honest. Let your answer have integrity!)

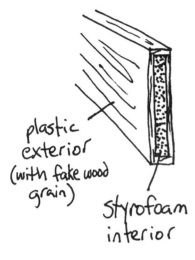

plastic exterior (with fake wood grain)

styrofoam interior

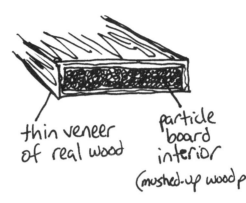

thin veneer of real wood

particle board interior (mushed-up wood pulp)

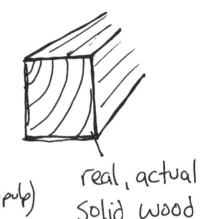

real, actual solid wood

2. Check all the areas of your life that cause an integrity struggle.

- ❏ Not telling the truth (lying)
- ❏ Pretending to be different than I am
- ❏ Changing my mind
- ❏ Breaking promises
- ❏ Not being there for my friends when they need me
- ❏ Cheating
- ❏ Giving people the answer I think they want to hear
- ❏ Other:_____

3. The one area from question 2 that I really want God's help to change is—

4. What can I do? What are some ideas for how I can grow in this area?

5. What will I do? What will I try this week?

6. What have I done? How, in the last week, have I been untrustworthy, and how can I fix it?

38

God is like a
POTTER

Yet, O Lord, you are our Father. We are the clay, you are the potter; we are all the work of your hand. Isaiah 64:8

GOALS

Students will—

* Understand why God is like a potter
* Understand how they can be like a potter when they choose to influence others in a positive way
* Write out a plan for how they will try to influence someone toward God and good stuff

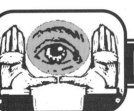

Picture Prep

Molding

When talking about God the Potter molding us, there's really nothing that compares to playing with some molding clay to get a tactile feel of the molding process. I know it's a little work, but if you make, buy, or borrow enough molding clay for each kid to have a little wad, you'll take them a long way in their understanding of this picture of God.

You'll need—
* molding clay for everyone

Here are a couple of easy ways to play with the clay. And I suggest you do both of them, if you have time.

First, break the kids into teams (three kids, maybe four) and have a molding contest. Give them three minutes to combine their clay and make one sculpture. The only rule is that everyone has to be involved in the molding process. After they're done, you can judge the sculptures based on originality and quality.

Now combine groups so you only have two to four groups altogether. It's time to play Play-Doh Pictionary. This game is played like Pictionary or *Win, Lose, or Draw* (the television show) but with clay. You have a list of words (below). Representatives from the teams come to you to get the word for that round. Then they go back to their teams and mold it for them. They're not allowed to talk or make any noise at all. And it's not charades—they can't act it out with their bodies, they can only use the clay itself. Once their team guesses the correct answer, end that round and have new reps come up and get the next word. Here are some words you can use.

* **tooth**
* **elephant**
* **drum**
* **pear**
* **tree**
* **bus**
* **church**
* **God** (This one's just for fun—it will be almost impossible to get the answer without cheating.)

Best Modeling Clay (à la Play-Doh)

Mix in a medium pot—
  1 cup flour
  ¼ cup salt
  2 tbs. cream of tartar

Combine and add—
  1 cup water
  2 tsp. food coloring
  1 tbs. oil

Cook over medium heat and stir about 3-5 minutes. It will look like a globby mess, and you'll be sure it's not turning out, but it will! When it forms a ball in the center of the pot, remove and knead on a lightly floured surface. Store in an airtight container.

The no-time-to-cook version

Mix together—
  1 cup flour
  ½ cup salt
  2 tbs. oil
  1 tsp. alum
Slowly add a small amount of water until the dough has the consistency you want.

Human Molding

If there's no way you can get some molding clay (maybe because you began preparing for this lesson seven minutes before it's scheduled to begin?), you can use this alternate opening. Or, if you have lots of time, you can use them both.

You'll need—
• no materials

If your group is 12 or fewer kids, divide them into two teams. If your group is larger than 12, still divide them into two teams, but choose four representatives from each team to come to the front. Name the teams, or call them Team 1 and Team 2. Have Team 2 face the opposite direction so they can't see Team 1. Then have Team 1 move three of their players into an inter-connected piece of modern art. Have them strike this pose (the nonposing person can help get them into place) and hold it.

Now designate a molder on Team 2. When you say, "Go!" the molder turns around and looks at the human modern art form that Team 1 has created. The molder then has to move her other three teammates into a mirror image of Team 1's pose. The teammates can only move how she moves them but can hold whatever pose she puts them in. Keep track of the time it takes for Team 2 to finish.

Then trade roles—Team 1 looks the other way while Team 2 poses. Then a molder from Team 1 moves his teammates into a mirror image. Again, keep track of the time.

Play as many rounds as the kids want to play—but probably about three rounds, rotating the molder (and the entire team if you want) each time. Add up the times and declare a winning team.

Action shot

Molding Stories

Make a transition by describing the process of throwing pottery. If you've never seen this done, here's a description.

Hundred to One Ain't Good

To say small groups are important in junior high ministry is like saying snow is important to winter. Junior highers interact in small groups differently than high school students, however. Issues of discipline, self-image, and gender can send a discussion careening off the topic.

Trial and error taught me two good student-to-leader ratios for junior high small groups—6 to 1 and 10 to 2. One adult leader can effectively lead a small group of about six young teens; a group that grows past six works better with two adult leaders. My *best* format for a junior high small group is about 10 kids with two leaders. One leader teaches while the other one polices and supports. And they won't have to find substitutes since one can cover for the other.

Finally, small groups with young teens always function more smoothly if they're made up of only one gender.

From Help! I'm a Junior High Youth Worker! *by Mark Oestreicher (Youth Specialties).*

The potter has a big cement wheel, turned on its side. It's connected to another wheel at his feet. He spins the lower wheel with his feet to keep the top wheel spinning. Then he takes a lump of clay and throws it down, hard, onto the middle of the wheel where it sticks to some little grips. With wet hands, he must first center the clay. He pushes and shoves and works the clay to get it spinning right in the center of the wheel. If it's not in the center, it can fly off and collapse. After the clay is centered, he begins to mold it—often with his hands, sometimes with tools. It doesn't happen all at once—it takes time. He has to squish it and rough it up. He stretches and pulls. He pours more water on it to keep it wet and moldable. When he's happy with the pottery, he stops the wheel

You'll need—
• Bibles
• enough copies of **Molding Stories** (page 43-44) so you'll have one strip for every two kids

and pulls off the clay piece very carefully. It's still very fragile and could collapse under its own weight very easily. Eventually, he puts it in a furnace to bake. Only then is the beautiful and useful piece of pottery complete.

Ask, **How is this like what God does with us?** [He molds us and changes us into the people he wants us to be. It's not always easy—sometimes he has to push hard. But in the end we can be beautiful and useful for his purposes.]

Now have your students get into pairs. Assign each pair one of the following molding stories from the Bible, by handing them a strip cut from a copy of **Molding Stories** on page 43. Instruct the pairs to read the story, then answer the question on their slips—"How did God mold this person?"

Gideon
Judges 6:11-16
How did God mold Gideon?
This is the great story of God seeing what Gideon *could* be, not what Gideon was. God, through his angel, approaches Gideon while he's hiding, afraid for his life. God greets him as a mighty warrior and goes on to prove that, with God, he is!

David
2 Samuel 12:1-13
How did God mold David?
This is the passage after David sins with Bathsheba and has her husband Uriah killed. Nathan confronts David about his sin. God uses Nathan to mold and convince David to own up to his sin.

Peter
Matthew 16:13-20
How did God mold Peter?
This classic passage shows Jesus calling Peter "the rock." Peter had not been acting like a rock. He'd been a wishy-washy, impulsive guy. Not only does God show him what he'll become, but Jesus also molds him into a strong and sturdy person.

Sarah
Genesis 18:1-2, 9-15; 21:1-7
How did God mold Sarah?
Sarah laughed! She thought it was downright funny that God had promised her a baby from her own womb when she was this old. The first time she'd laughed, it was laughter of joy. But 10 years later when God made his promise again, she laughed again and this time her laughter seemed more skeptical. But God molds her, even in this encounter with the angel, and keeps his promise by molding her into a mom!

Give the groups about three or four minutes to complete their task, while you roam around the room making sure they stay on task (yeah, right!) Then pull the group back together and have at least one group from each story share a summary of what they read and their conclusions about God the Potter.

Conclude this section by asking, **Okay, now that you've seen God the Potter in action, tell me some of the ways he does this molding in peoples' lives.** [He allows us to go through tough situations, allows us to live with hard and unanswered questions, brings people into our lives who challenge us—in good ways and bad ways, lets us suffer the consequences of our sins even when he'd love to take them away.]

Transition into this next section by saying, **With each of these pictures of God we're looking at, we're spending time understanding why God used this description of himself. But then we want to turn the camera around and point it at ourselves. Since we're God's children, his DNA should be in us. And that means these pictures should be pictures of us too!**

Then ask, **So how can you and I be like a potter? Who do we mold? How do we do it?**

Self-portrait

The Great Debate

Divide your group into four teams. Then hand out copies of **The Great Debate** (page 45) to each student. This sheet contains stories about four kids. Each one tells about a teen having a molding influence on someone else. Read through all four stories together. If you've got four good readers (two guys and two girls), have them read the stories. Putting them in the voice of a young teen will make them more believable.

Now assign one story to each team. Instruct them that you're going to ask for one member of each team to come up front and be part of a debate. The team's task is to defend the character in its story as the best example of a student-potter. They should take a few minutes to discuss

the team's strategy and choose a debater. This person might want to jot down some notes in preparation for the debate.

After a couple minutes, ask the four representatives to come up to the chairs in front. Give each of them one minute to argue why her character is the best potter. After all four are finished, give them an opportunity to make comments about the other characters. Then let them all share any new thoughts about other ways their own characters could have influenced people. The goal here isn't really to decide which character is the best potter, as much as it is to get some thought going about what it takes to be a young teen people molder.

After the kids have had their say, say something like this, **Well, all four of the characters showed an example of a teen having a molding influence on another person. So they're all living out what we're talking about today.**

Print it!

My Influence

As you distribute a 3x5 card and pencil or pen to each student say, **What about you? Each of you has the ability to influence and mold people toward God, toward good stuff. We influence people all the time. The question is— are you going to make the choice to be a good influence or a bad influence? If you don't make a choice at all, you probably won't be a good influence.**

Now ask each student to spend 30 seconds in silence. Ask them to pray and ask God whom he would like them to influence. Then instruct them to write the name on their cards, along with a plan for how they're going to do this.

After a minute or two, have your students pull back into groups of three or four and share their answers with each other. After each person shares, the others in the group should give additional suggestions for how the student could influence someone in that situation. Tell kids to write down the ideas they're willing to try.

If your students can handle it, have them close in prayer in those groups, praying that God will continue to mold each of them and give them the courage to be molders for him.

HANDY REVIEW OPTION
Weekly Wall Art

If you've been using the signs idea described at the end of Lesson 1, add a graphic of a clay pot to your wall.

Molding Stories

Yet, O Lord, you are our Father. We are the clay, you are the potter; we are all the work of your hand. Isaiah 64:8

Gideon—Judges 6:11-16

The angel of the Lord came and sat down under the oak in Ophrah that belonged to Joash the Abiezrite, where his son Gideon was threshing wheat in a winepress to keep it from the Midianites. When the angel of the Lord appeared to Gideon, he said, "The Lord is with you, mighty warrior."

"But sir," Gideon replied, "if the Lord is with us, why has all this happened to us? Where are all his wonders that our fathers told us about when they said, 'Did not the Lord bring us up out of Egypt?' But now the Lord has abandoned us and put us into the hand of Midian."

The Lord turned to him and said, "Go in the strength you have and save Israel out of Midian's hand. Am I not sending you?"

"But Lord," Gideon asked, "how can I save Israel? My clan is the weakest in Manasseh, and I am the least in my family."

The Lord answered, "I will be with you, and you will strike down all the Midianites togther."

How did God mold Gideon?

Yet, O Lord, you are our Father. We are the clay, you are the potter; we are all the work of your hand.   Isaiah 64:8

David—2 Samuel 12:1-13

The Lord sent Nathan to David. When he came to him, he said, "There were two men in a certain town, one rich and the other poor. The rich man had a very large number of sheep and cattle, but the poor man had nothing except one little ewe lamb he had bought. He raised it, and it grew up with him and his children. It shared his food, drank from his cup and even slept in his arms. It was like a daughter to him. Now a traveler came to the rich man, but the rich man refrained from taking one of his own sheep or cattle to prepare a meal for the traveler who had come to him. Instead, he took the ewe lamb that belonged to the poor man and prepared it for the one who had come to him."

David burned with anger against the man and said to Nathan, "As surely as the Lord lives, the man who did this deserves to die! He must pay for that lamb four times over, because he did such a thing and had no pity."

Then Nathan said to David, "You are that man! This is what the Lord, the God of Israel, says: 'I anointed you king over Israel, and I delivered you from the hand of Saul. I gave your master's house to you, and your master's wives into your arms. I gave you the house of Israel and Judah. And if all this had been too little, I would have given you even more. Why did you despise the word of the Lord by doing what is evil in his eyes? You struck down Uriah the Hittite with the sword and took his wife to be your own. You killed him with the sword of the Ammonites. Now, therefore, the sword will never depart from your house, because you despised me and took the wife of Uriah the Hittite to be your own.'

"This is what the Lord says: 'Out of your own household I am going to bring calamity upon you. Before your very eyes I will take your wives and give them to one who is close to you, and he will lie with your wives in broad daylight. You did it in secret, but I will do this thing in broad daylight before all Israel.'"

Then David said to Nathan, "I have sinned against the Lord."

Nathan replied, "The Lord has taken away your sin. You are not going to die."

How did God mold David?

43

Yet, O Lord, you are our Father. We are the clay, you are the potter; we are all the work of your hand. Isaiah 64:8

Peter—Matthew 16:13-20

When Jesus came to the region of Caesarea Philippi, he asked his disciples, "Who do people say the Son of Man is?"

They replied, "Some say John the Baptist; others say Elijah; and still others, Jeremiah or one of the prophets."

"But what about you?" he asked. "Who do you say I am?"

Simon Peter answered, "You are the Christ, the Son of the living God."

Jesus replied, "Blessed are you, Simon son of Jonah, for this was not revealed to you by man, but by my Father in heaven. And I tell you that you are Peter, and on this rock I will build my church, and the gates of Hades will not overcome it. I will give you the keys of the kingdom of heaven; whatever you bind on earth will be bound in heaven, and whatever you loose on earth will be loosed in heaven." Then he warned his disciples not to tell anyone that he was the Christ.

How did God mold Peter?

Yet, O Lord, you are our Father. We are the clay, you are the potter; we are all the work of your hand. Isaiah 64:8

Sarah—Genesis 18:1-2, 9-15; 21:1-7

The Lord appeared to Abraham near the great trees of Mamre while he was sitting at the entrance to his tent in the heat of the day. Abraham looked up and saw three men standing nearby. When he saw them, he hurried from the entrance of his tent to meet them and bowed low to the ground...

"Where is your wife Sarah?" they asked him.

"There in the tent," he said.

Then the Lord said, "I will surely return to you about this time next year, and Sarah your wife will have a son."

Now Sarah was listening at the entrance to the tent, which was behind him. Abraham and Sarah were already old and well advanced in years, and Sarah was past the age of childbearing. So Sarah laughed to herself as she thought, "After I am worn out and my master is old, will I now have this pleasure?"

Then the Lord said to Abraham, "Why did Sarah laugh and say, 'Will I really have a child, now that I am old?' Is anything too hard for the Lord? I will return to you at the appointed time next year and Sarah will have a son."

Sarah was afraid, so she lied and said, "I did not laugh."

But he said, "Yes, you did laugh." ...

Now the Lord was gracious to Sarah as he had said, and the Lord did for Sarah what he had promised. Sarah became pregnant and bore a son to Abraham in his old age, at the very time God had promised him. Abraham gave the name Isaac to the son Sarah bore him. When his son Isaac was eight days old, Abraham circumcised him, as God commanded him. Abraham was a hundred years old when his son Isaac was born to him.

Sarah said, "God has brought me laughter, and everyone who hears about this will laugh with me." And she added, "Who would have said to Abraham that Sarah would nurse children? Yet I have borne him a son in his old age."

How did God mold Sarah?

44

The Great Debate

Team 1
Your character: Kenny
His story: Kenny has been playing basketball for a long time, and he's really good. His teammates totally look to him for direction and example. He decides he's going to take this shaping and molding stuff seriously. So he asks his coach if he can be the team chaplain and starts reading a Bible verse and praying before every game.

Team 2
Your character: Amy
Her story: Amy hangs out all the time with Kristi, who's constantly trying to get attention. In fact, Kristi will do just about anything for attention, including going along with the crowd or saying things just to shock people. Amy decides to try to have a molding influence on Kristi by doing two things: she'll make sure Kristi knows she can count on Amy to be her friend no matter what, and she'll take the gutsy step of talking to Kristi about her attention-getting behavior.

Team 3
Your character: Cory
His story: Cory's family used to go to church all the time when he was a kid. But for whatever reason—weekends out of town, extra work at the office—his parents don't go anymore. However, his family has this tradition that each weekend a different family member gets to choose one thing they will do together. He and his sister usually choose a movie or going out for ice cream. Then Cory uses up all his turns for a year in one statement. He says, "For the rest of this year, every time it's my turn I choose that we go to church together as a family."

Team 4
Your character: Jaci
Her story: Jaci's group of friends are really nice girls. They all go to the same school and the same youth group. They're even willing to let other people hang out with them. There's only one problem—they gossip like crazy! Every evening they're on the phone with each other sharing rumors and stories, trashing people, and talking about them behind their backs. Well Jaci's had enough of it, and thinks it's time she tried to influence and mold this group a bit. So she has them all spend the night at her house, then tells them, "This is the coolest group of friends, but this gossip thing is out of control. It's wrong, and I wish you would all stop. But I can only control what I do and say, so I'm telling you now that I won't listen to or pass on gossip any more."

45

God is like a SERVANT

Here is my servant, whom I uphold, my chosen one in whom I delight; I will put my Spirit on him and he will bring justice to the nations.

Isaiah 42:1

GOALS

Students will—

- Understand why God is like a servant
- Understand that they are imitating God when they serve others
- Choose a gutsy act of service

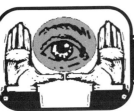

Picture Prep

Championship Serving

Divide your group into teams of, well, that depends on the size of your group. If you have a small group (a dozen or less), use teams of two or three. If your group is larger, use larger groups. About six kids per group is the largest they should be.

You'll need—
- a prize for the winning team (a bag of candy)
- a impartial judge

Tell them you're going to give them about three minutes to come up with a plan for serving another group or person in this room. However, they have to do the serving here and now. Introduce your judge and show the prize. Tell them they'll be judged on participation, attitude, and creativity. And they're not allowed to serve the judge. (This judge does not allow bribery!)

Now before you start muttering to yourself, "This is the stupidest opening exercise I've ever read! Servanthood is much deeper than this trivial stuff!"—yeah, yeah, I fully agree with you. Lighten up. You're going to make that point later, okay?

This is just setting the stage.

Give the groups three minutes or so to come up with a plan. If you don't have too many groups, have them perform their act of service one group at a time so they can all watch each other. Otherwise the judge will really have to keep his eyes open!

After they've all served someone else, have the judge pronounce a winning group and award them some kind of prize, like a bag of candy or a new car.

Now ask—

- **What was wrong with the service we just did?** *[It was forced, not voluntary, so it wasn't really service! And winning a prize tainted the motive. So, again, it wasn't really serving as much as competing for a prize.]*
- **In a wealthy house or a king's castle, what does a servant do?** *[Uh, serves?]*
- **So, what does it mean to serve? What's a definition of servanthood?** *[To offer your services—things you can do—to someone else for their benefit.]*

SERVICE PROJECT
Get Your Hands Dirty

If you're going to teach a lesson on servanthood, there's no better context than right after your students have been involved in the act of serving. So plan a service project for a Saturday, if you're planning to teach this lesson on a Sunday morning; or meet a little early for your youth group and let the kids get their hands dirty by helping others.

Here are some ideas for you.

- **Clean up trash in a community park.**
- **Rake leaves, shovel snow, plant flowers, or wash windows for elderly people (in your church or just in your neighborhood).**
- **Run a free car wash—refuse to accept donations.**
- **Hand out cold soft drinks to people in rush hour traffic on a hot day.**
- **Volunteer to help at a homeless shelter or soup kitchen.**
- **Offer free babysitting to parents of young kids.**
- **And if you can't think of anything else and live in the San Diego area, I've got some work you can do on my house!**

Make a transition by saying, **The Bible calls God a servant. How is this true?** Don't worry if you get incomplete answers here—it's just a set-up question to the Scripture work they're about to embark on.

Serving Stories

It's time to catch Jesus in the act of serving. Hand out copies of **Serving Stories** (page 51) and pens or pencils to all your students.

Tell them you want them to work in pairs and pick two stories from the top of the page. (You could assign the stories or have students pick them out loud to verify that they're all taken.)

They should look up the story in the Bible, read

it, then answer the questions at the bottom of the page.

Give the pairs about five to seven minutes to complete this work. As always, you should move around the room to mock kids who write dumb answers—no wait, that's not it. Move around the room to rough up the kid who's goofing off—no, wait, that's not it either. Oh yeah, move around the room to make sure they understand what they're supposed to be doing. Yeah, that's it.

After the pairs seem to have completed their work, pull the group back together and ask for answers from the different stories.

You'll notice I put a difficult question in each section of the worksheet, "Why did Jesus serve?" Kids will probably struggle with this one and may not come up with an answer. That's okay. It's good for them to wrestle with this kind of abstract question. The answer is, in adult language, Jesus serves because he's God; and God's nature is to serve—it comes from his overwhelming propensity to love us. In kid language the answer is "Jesus serves because he loves us."

Have your students look at the passage printed at the top of their wildpages (Matthew 20:26b-28a).

Then ask—

- **How is what Jesus says here different from most of the world?** [*Most of our world says, "Claw your way to the top—look out for yourself." The idea of becoming number one by serving people seems backward.*]
- **What's so amazing about the fact that God serves us?** [*He's God! He could just rule us. There's no reason why serving us would benefit him.*]
- **What can we learn about servant-hood from God?** [*This is a tougher question. The answers are along the same lines as the last question—we learn that the best servanthood is done without a selfish motive. We learn that serving people flows out of our love for them. We learn that it doesn't make you a wuss to serve people.*]

Simon Sez

Make a transition by playing an old-fashioned game of *Simon Says*. Change the name of the game to your own name, though (*Mark Says*). Have all your kids stand up. Instruct them that they're to do whatever you say when it's preceded by "_____ says."

If they do what you say when you don't say "_____ says," then they have to sit down. All your kids have played this game at some point in their lives, so they'll know the rules.

Begin with easy instructions and move to more difficult. Trap kids by—

- doing what you're describing, when you say to stop doing something and you also stop doing it without saying Simon says—they'll follow your example
- giving directions very quickly, several in a row, with a catch at the end
- using an extremely casual tone of voice
- setting them up with actions that are hard to sustain and catch lines that will force them out

Here's a sample list of instructions you can use.

Insert your own name.

- **Mark says yawn loudly.**
- **Mark says clap your hands.**
- **Clap them again.** (sit down?)
- **Mark says clap your hands.**
- **Mark says clap your hands.**
- **Mark says clap your hands.**
- **Mark says clap your hands.**
- **Clap your hands.** (sit down?)
- **Mark says give the person next to you a high-five.**
- **Mark says give them a low-five.**
- **Then give 'em a side-five.** (sit down?)
- **Mark says jump up and down.**
- **Mark says keep jumping up and down.** (pause)
- **Okay, you can stop.** (sit down?)
- **Mark says stand on one leg.**
- **Mark says don't put the other leg down.**
- **Mark says if you put it down you're out!**
- **Mark says hop on your one leg.**
- **Mark says clap while you continue hopping.**
- **Mark says blink your eyes while you clap and hop on one leg.**
- **Mark says say, "I look strange" over and over again, while continuing to blink, clap, and hop on one leg.**
- **Okay, stop clapping, but keep doing all the other things.** (sit down?)
- **Mark says stop everything.**
- **Mark says when I say "Go!" jump up in the air real high.**
- **"Go!"** (sit down?)
- **Mark says when I say "Go!" jump up in the air real high**
- **Mark says "Go."**
- **Come back down.** (everyone remaining will now be out!)

Say, **You did a pretty good job of imitating me. So let me tell you the big truth of the day. Ready? You act the most like God when you imitate him and serve people.**

Say that last sentence a couple times, then put it in first person and have the kids repeat it with you a couple times. (It would be great if you had this sentence on an overhead or a whiteboard: I ACT THE MOST LIKE GOD WHEN I IMITATE HIM AND SERVE PEOPLE.)

If you have a few extra minutes, you can have

some fun as you help your students commit this to memory. Have kids pair up and try saying the sentence as fast as they can, while alternating words between the two of them. See if there's a pair of kids who can do it really fast. If you have a larger group, you could see if 13 girls can line up and say the sentence (one word per student) faster than 13 guys. Or pit seventh graders against eighth graders.

Print it!

My Serve

Pass out copies of **My Serve!** (page 52) to your students. Actually, it would be great if you could copy them back-to-back with **Serving Stories**—although, undoubtedly, some kids will have destroyed those by now.

Work through the first question together.

You'll need—
- copies of **My Serve!** (page 52)
- pens or pencils

Have kids check off their answers but ask some of them to respond out loud. Then give them a couple minutes to work on the second question. After a few minutes, you might want to ask if a few will share what they picked.

Close in prayer by thanking God for serving us and asking him to give us the courage to serve others.

HANDY REVIEW OPTION
Weekly Wall Art

If you've been using the signs idea described at the end of Lesson 1, add a graphic of a white-gloved arm with a towel over it. (You know—a butler-servant's arm!)

Serving Stories

Whoever wants to become great among you must be your servant, and whoever wants to be first must be your slave—just as the Son of Man did not come to be served, but to serve.
Matthew 20:26-28

Catch Jesus in the act of serving. You and a partner pick two of these stories. Look 'em up in the Bible. Read 'em. Then answer the questions below.

Matthew 1:18-25—Jesus' birth
Matthew 4:23-25 and 8:14-17—Jesus healing people
Matthew 8:5-13—Jesus and the Centurion
Matthew 9:18-26—A dead girl and a sick woman

Matthew 14:13-21—Jesus feeds a big ol' crowd
Matthew 14:22-33—Jesus surfs out to the disciples
Matthew 27:45-54—Jesus' death

Story 1 _____

Whom did Jesus serve in this story?

How did he serve them?

Why did he do it? (tough question)

Story 2 _____

Whom did Jesus serve in this story?

How did he serve them?

Why did he do it? (tough question)

My Serve!

What keeps you from serving? (Be honest!)

❑ I'm selfish.
❑ I don't feel like it.
❑ It means I have to think about other people.
❑ I don't get anything for it.
❑ It's inconvenient.
❑ I'd rather have them serve me.
❑ I don't usually think of it.
❑ I don't know.
❑ Another reason: _____

What will you do this week to imitate Jesus the Servant?

❑ I'll serve my parents by doing the jobs I'm supposed to do around the house without grumbling.
❑ I'll serve my sister or brother by helping them with one of their chores—or even doing it for them (without expecting anything in return).
❑ I'll serve one of my friends by listening to her without interrupting all the time.
❑ I'll serve one of my friends by offering to help him with something he doesn't want to do.
❑ I'll serve God by obeying him. I'll do this in this specific area: _____
❑ I'll serve an older person on my street by doing some free yard work for her.
❑ I'll serve a homeless person by bringing him some food.
❑ Another serving plan: _____

God is like an INVENTOR

(Lesson 7)

You made the heavens, even the highest heavens, and all their starry host, the earth and all that is on it, the seas and all that is in them.

Nehemiah 9:6b

GOALS

Students will—

- Understand why God is like an inventor
- Understand how they can be like an inventor by using the creative gifts God gave them
- Reflect on their inventiveness and write ideas for how to use it more often

Picture Prep

Make Something

Begin by showing your group an invention or two that you really like, something that makes your life just a little better. This could be anything from your electric razor to your favorite pen to the bib that really catches your baby's drool. For me it would be my coffee grinder and my favorite fountain pen. Nothing amazing here—nothing kids haven't seen before. You're just setting up the idea of inventing.

Divide students into groups of three to six. Instruct them that their task is to invent something. The only criterion is that the thing should somehow make the daily life of a junior higher easier. Once they think of something, they should draw a big picture of it on the piece of butcher paper or posterboard.

Give the groups about five minutes to complete their work. Then have them present their inventions

You'll need—
- large pieces of butcher paper or posterboard
- markers
- an example or two of inventions that you really like

to the whole group, one at a time. Make sure you affirm their work.

Action shot

Creation Sound Effects

Ask some questions—

- **What invention do you think is pretty amazing?**
- **What do you wish someone would invent?**
- **What cool inventions have you heard about that people are working on right now?**
- **What, in your opinion, is the most amazing invention of all time?**

(It'll be interesting to see if kids just say things like

You'll need—
- one copy of **Creation Sound Effects** (page 56) for yourself

53

the car or the airplane. Don't be shocked if some sharp but quiet home-schooled kid comes up with the real answer—people.)

Now tell your group that they have the assignment of being a sound effects team. You're going to read a paraphrased version of the story of creation, from Genesis, chapter 1; and every time you point to them you want them to provide the appropriate sound effects.

Read **Creation Sound Effects** (page 56). (Read it out loud once or twice before your group meets so you can read it well.) Every time you see this symbol ◆, pause and point to your group until they provide an appropriate sound effect. The sound effects are fairly obvious and easy once the creation of animals gets going but it calls for a little more creativity at the beginning. Push your kids to be creative.

After you've read the story, ask these questions—

- **So what's the most amazing invention of all time?** [Us!]
- **Which of God's other inventions do you think took a lot of creativity?**
- **Here's the big tough question: Why? Why did God create all this stuff?** [You could have a major theological debate on this, but the short answer is—it's his nature to create.]

Self-portrait

Inventors-R-Us

Remind your students of the point of this series of lessons: if these pictures of God are accurate (which they are) and if we're children of God, then some of the DNA of those pictures must be in us as well.

Ask four volunteers to come forward—two

Love Roller Coaster

As junior highers begin to think abstractly, they experience new emotions and old emotions in new ways. This throws them into the most topsy-turvy, hot-and-cold time of their lives.

A young teen's experience of a romantic breakup, for example, is as real as an adult's more mature response to similar pain. Although adults downplay the teen's emotional trauma by saying, "You don't really know what love is yet," that junior higher's emotion at that moment is deeper than any they've ever known.

God made junior highers this way—and everything God makes is good. So enjoy their roller coaster vicariously. This emotional field-tripping can be fun! Just make sure your seat belt is strapped securely across your lap.

From *Help! I'm a Junior High Youth Worker!* by Mark Oestreicher (Youth Specialties).

guys and two girls. (It would be good to select these kids ahead of time and to let them look over their assigned paragraphs so they can prepare a bit.) Without making it somehow obvious and hurting anyone's feelings, try to choose kids who won't be embarrassed by their reading ability. Asking poor readers to read publicly can be 10 times worse for them than not being asked to read.

Give each volunteer a copy of **Inventors-R-Us** (page 57); and ask them to read their pretend stories, one at a time. (It wouldn't be very profitable to have them all read at once, now would it?) After each story is read, pause and then lead a discussion with the whole group, using these questions as a starting point:

You'll need—
- four copies of **Inventors-R-Us** (page 57)
- four volunteer kids (two guys and two girls) to read the stories

- **How is _____ (name of character) like an inventor?**
- **How could they use their inventor ability even more?**
- **How could they use their inventor ability for God?**

(This is kind of a trick question—maybe even for you! We should be careful that we don't teach our kids that their creative abilities are only good when used in Christian work. Utilizing their inventive abilities in the way God intended them to be used—any way that is not evil or sinful—*is* honoring to God. When we use our gifts and abilities, we honor him. When a cellist plays the cello, it doesn't have to be Christian cello music for that creative act to be honoring to God. When an architect designs a building, doing so with the awareness that God gave him that ability means he's using his inventiveness to God's glory. Get it? This is a bit paradigm-shaking for many of us who grew up in the church believing that Christian work was the best or only way to glorify God. Make sure you help your students understand this. Okay, I've preached my sermon—back to your lesson!)

The whole idea of this section is to get your kids thinking about the huge variety of inventive abilities that exist. When it comes to application, it's easier and safer for young teens to think in third person before they think in first person. So this section is really just setting up the personal application to come. (By the way, you'll find that's true in most of these lessons.)

own. Encourage them to answer the questions with an attitude of prayer, asking God to help them with the answers.

If your kids are spread out during this task, quietly walk around so they can ask you questions if they have them, but don't interrupt them. After about seven to ten minutes, pull them back together and have a few willing kids share their conclusions.

Don't forget to close in prayer, thanking God for inventing us and asking him for wisdom to see our inventiveness and put it into practice in a way that will honor him.

HANDY REVIEW OPTION
Weekly Wall Art

If you're using the signs idea described at the end of Lesson 1, add a graphic to your wall to signify this picture—maybe a graphic of the world (to symbolize God's creation).

Yes, I *Am* an Inventor

Pass out half-sheet copies of **Yes, I *Am* an Inventor** (page 58) and pens or pencils to your students. Tell them to work individually on this sheet. If you're not confined to a small room, it would be great to give kids a little solitude on this one. Have them find a place where they can work alone for 10 minutes without distractions. However, this may not be possible for you. (Teaching your junior high group in the janitor's closet, are you?) You can still encourage kids to ignore all distractions and work on their

You'll need—
- copies of **Yes, I *Am* an Inventor** (page 58) cut in half
- pens or pencils

Creation Sound Effects

In the beginning there was nothing, ◆ and God decided to make earth. First he said, "Let there be light." And there was light. ◆ And God separated the light and the darkness, and there was night, and then the first morning. ◆

Then God made land ◆ and separated it from the water, ◆ and separated both of them from the sky. ◆ On top of the land he added plants of all kinds—big trees ◆ and pretty little flowers. ◆

Then God got going with the animals! First he thought up fish. He made whales ◆ and dolphins ◆ and lobsters ◆ and other fish. ◆ Then he went for the skies. He made eagles ◆ and chickadees ◆ and hummingbirds ◆ and crows. ◆

Next, God invented the land animals. He thought up horses ◆ and cows ◆ and chickens ◆ and frogs. ◆ He created pigs ◆ and dogs ◆ and elephants ◆ and donkeys. ◆ He even made lions ◆ and lizards ◆ and monkeys ◆ and hyenas. ◆ Can you imagine what it sounded like when all these animals made their noises together for the first time? ◆

Then God rolled up his sleeves and did his most amazing work. He invented a man ◆ and a woman. ◆

Altogether, it was a pretty impressive group of inventions!

End

Inventors-R-Us

Story 1

Shelly

Hi! I'm Shelly. I've always liked to draw, but it wasn't until last year in art class that I started to realize I'm pretty good at it. Some people who paint or draw like to look at a picture or a person or something outdoors and try to draw or paint it just like they see it. They're kind of like photographers who use paint or pencils instead of a camera. But that's not how I like to draw. I like to close my eyes and think. I picture in my mind some scene or shape or maybe even just a bunch of colors and then start to draw. I'm never totally sure what the drawing is going to end up looking like because I kind of create it as I go along.

Story 2

James

Hey, I'm James. My parents got me my first computer when I was four because I spent so much time on my dad's computer that he couldn't use it! For a long time all I did was play games and talk in chat rooms and stuff. But a couple years ago I started to write some simple programs. At first it was goofy stuff, like a program to help my little sister organize her Beanie Babies. But now that I know how to do it better, I've been doing harder stuff. A few months ago I helped put together a program for my dad's office that keeps track of all their delivery trucks. And right now I'm working on a Web site for my dad's company.

Story 3

Shana

My name's Shana. Some people think it's strange for a junior higher, but I'm really into plants and flowers and stuff. Not just looking at them, but growing them. It started with a little row of flowers outside my bedroom window; but now I've got stuff growing all around our house, inside and outside. I never read any books or took any classes or anything. And I killed off a bunch of plants before I learned how to make them really grow. Sometimes they still die because I'm always trying to figure out ways to make them grow bigger and stronger. You should see this tomato plant I've got growing in my backyard right now—the tomatoes are huge!

Story 4

Zack

Hey, I'm Zack. I'm not an artist like Shelly or a computer whiz like James or a gardener like Shana. It's hard to put a name to what I like to do. My mom calls it problem solving. I used to get those game magazines and try to figure out the answers to the tricky questions and riddles. But now I've found that I'm pretty good at helping people figure out good answers to tricky questions and riddles in the real world. Like last week, Shana was talking to me about her tomato plant, and I thought of an idea that she should try. It's not that I know much about tomato plants or anything. I just listened to what she told me, put the pieces together in my head, and came up with an idea. It's kind of funny because my uncle calls me all the time with questions about problems at his factory. I love trying to come up with solutions.

57

WILDPAGE

Yes, I *Am* an Inventor!

1. In what way am I like an inventor?

2. One or two God-given abilities that I could use to be inventive are—

3. This is one way I've used these already— (It's okay if you don't have an answer to this question.)

4. One way I can use these abilities in a way that would honor God is—

- -

WILDPAGE

Yes, I *Am* an Inventor!

1. In what way am I like an inventor?

2. One or two God-given abilities that I could use to be inventive are—

3. This is one way I've used these already— (It's okay if you don't have an answer to this question.)

4. One way I can use these abilities in a way that would honor God is—

58

God is like a
MOM

As a mother comforts her child, so will I comfort you. Isaiah 66:13a

GOALS

Students will—

- Understand their ability to influence people in good ways or bad ways.

- Choose a specific way they will influence someone toward right living in the next week.

Picture Prep

Mom Cheer

You'll need—
- no materials

Divide your group into teams of three to ten, depending on the size of your group. Instruct the teams that they'll have five minutes to put together a cheer for moms. It should include why moms are good or some of their good qualities. It can't be, "Gimme an M!" Ideally, the teams will have somewhere to work where the other groups won't hear them; but if that's not possible, don't worry about it. After about five minutes, have each team perform their cheer.

Then ask these questions—

- **What makes a good mom?**
- **What are important qualities of a mom?**

OPTIONAL CORRESPONDENCE
Letters from Mom

Ask a few moms to write anonymous letters about what's good and what's hard about being a mom. Solicit these a couple weeks in advance. That way they'll have a week to get the letter written and delivered to you, and you'll have another week to decide what parts you'll use—just the parts that will connect with your kids. Highlight the parts you want to read.

You'll need—
- letters from a few moms

Action shot

Just Like Mom

Transition by saying something like, **This is not really a lesson about moms! It's a lesson about**

You'll need—
- copies of **Just Like Mom** (page 62)
- pens or pencils
- Bibles

God. One of the pictures God uses in the Bible to help us get to know him better is the picture of a mom. This might seem strange to you at first, but when you think of the good qualities of a mom—someone who looks out for you, protects you, and comforts you—that's what God also does for you!

Now pass out copies of **Just Like Mom** (page 62) and pens or pencils. Make sure kids either have their own Bibles or have access to one nearby. Allow kids to work in pairs to try to match up the verses in the left column with the mom-like characteristics in the right column. Explain that all these verses are talking about God, so they're all snapshots of this "God is like a Mom" picture. (The answers, by the way, are— e, a, f, c, b, d.)

After kids have had about three minutes to complete the work, read the descriptions and have kids shout out their answers. Lightheartedly ask if anyone spent time looking for the book of Hezitations—of course, in a way that won't embarrass anyone. Congratulate those who got them all right.

Ask, **So, now that we've looked at the qualities of a good mom and these**

snapshots of God—how would you say God is like a mom?** [He protects us, he offers comfort, he enjoys us.]

Then say something like, **Okay, for some of you, understanding that God is like a mom was probably something new— something you'd never thought of. Well get ready because that's only the first step. In these lessons, remember that whatever characteristics we see in God we should also catch glimpses of these traits in ourselves because we're children of God. That means all of us can be like moms too! This may not be a radical thought for some of you girls, but you guys have probably never thought of yourselves as moms!**

Self-portrait

Help Me Be a Mom!

Ask, **How do you think a young teen, someone without any children, can be like a mom?** (Your kids will probably think in concrete terms and suggest things like when you baby-sit children or play with your younger cousins. If they answer that way, say something like, **It's not that you can only be like a mom with little kids. You can be like a mom for people your own age and even older people! How's that?**) [The real answer goes right back to the descriptions in the right column of the **Just Like Mom** wildpage they just completed—we are like moms when we protect, comfort, and take joy in others.]

Now distribute copies of **Help Me Be a Mom!** (page 63) or ask your kids to turn their sheets over, if you copied them back-to-back.

> ### You'll need—
> - copies of **Help Me Be a Mom!** (page 63) (Since this exercise takes place right after they've used the **Just Like Mom** handouts, it would be good if you had the two wildpages photocopied back-to-back.)
> - pens or pencils

You could proceed with this in a couple of ways. If your kids don't mind writing and don't instantly destroy any handout you give them (are you sure you're working with junior highers? Are you sure they're alive?), then you could have them complete this sheet in the same pairs in which they completed the last worksheet. Debrief their answers after they've all written some things down. This is ideal in many ways because it allows kids an opportunity to think for themselves before they hear a bunch of other answers.

On the other hand, if writing a few letters on the first handout is about all your kids can handle ("Hey, hey, welcome to the wonderful world of junior high ministry—your group is just like the rest of ours!"), then just give them this handout so they can follow along while you read it and lead a discussion from up front.

Either way, read or have them read the stories on the page. Then ask them to advise the character on how he or she could be like a mom. For your information, the three stories are fairly broad, but in general terms—

• the first story hints at Kerry providing warm, caring protection
• the second story hints at Kirsten remembering someone she cares about and trying not to hurt her friend's feelings
• the third story hints at Raphael providing comfort for his friend Darren

comfort, care, or just knowing that you remember them. Give kids about a minute to do this.

Then have them turn their cards over and write a mom-plan for how they could be like a mom to this person in the next seven days. Finally, after another couple minutes, tell kids to circle their plan if they're willing to try it. Have a few kids share their plans. It would be best if you also had one of your own to share.

Reinforce your lesson as you close in prayer. Ask kids to thank God for being like a mom in our lives by mentioning the things he does. Then ask God to help everyone remember their mom plans.

HANDY REVIEW OPTION
Weekly Wall Art

If you're doing the signs idea described at the end of Lesson 1, add another graphic to your wall o' signs. This one could be a sign like the ones they have on the doors to women's restrooms—just a simple graphic of a woman.

i, Mom

While you're passing out 3x5 cards to your kids, say something like, **Okay, now it's time for you to get mom-like!**

Tell them to think for a minute then, on one side of the card, write the name of someone they know who would benefit from some protection,

Just Like Mom

Match the verses in the left column with the descriptions of a mom in the right column.

a. Isaiah 66:13

__ A good mom always protects her kids from bad stuff.

b. Psalm 5:11

__ A good mom provides comfort—hugs when you're sad, Band-Aids when you get hurt.

c. Isaiah 49:15

__ A good mom lets kids be kids. She doesn't try to make them act like little adults.

d. Hezitations 4:3

__ A good mom doesn't forget her kids, even after they're all grown up. She thinks about them all the time!

e. 2 Thessalonians 3:3

__ The kids of a good mom know they're safe, and it makes them so happy they could almost sing!

f. Matthew 19:13-15

__ This isn't a real passage in the Bible!

WiLDPAGE

Help Me Be a Mom!

My name's Kerry. I'm really big for my age, and kids seem to be afraid of me. They think I'm going to be a bully or something but I'm not. Anyhow, there's this kid at school that lots of kids pick on. His name's Timmy. He gets pushed around a lot, and kids like to trip him in the hallway and stuff. The other day Timmy and I ended up eating lunch at the same table. Neither of us meant to sit with the other—we just ended up there. Now I think he hopes I'll be his friend. How can I (wow, this is gonna sound weird!) be like a mom to Timmy?

I'm Kirsten. Two years ago I moved and left a really good friend of mine named Rachel. We e-mailed each other every day for a few months, but then I didn't answer her e-mails all the time. I was making new friends; and, to be honest, I kinda forgot about Rachel—until I'd get on my computer and see all these e-mails from her. I think I hurt her feelings. She's still an important friend to me, and I don't want to ignore her. How can I be like a mom to Rachel?

Hey, I'm Raphael. In my neighborhood you can get busted up for telling a guy he's like a girl. So this "be like a mom" stuff is pretty weird! Anyway, my friend Darren's life is kind of a mess right now. See, he never knew his dad until about a month ago. So his dad shows up and wants to be all buddy-buddy with him, which was fine with Darren. But then his dad took off again. And his mom—she doesn't seem to care at all, 'cause she can't stand Darren's dad. So Darren's pretty down about it. Usually I'd just ignore a friend's feelings and stuff—that's his business—but this "be like a mom" thing's kinda getting to me. Got any ideas for me?

God is like a
LISTENER

Before they call I will answer; while they are still speaking I will hear.

Isaiah 65:24

GOALS

Students will—

- Understand why God is like a listener
- Understand how they can be a listener when they—well, listen!
- Have an opportunity to approach someone in the room and commit to being a better listener

Picture Prep

Listen Up!

Divide your group into teams of three to eight, depending on the size of your group. Tell them their teams are going to compete in a listening competition. You're going to play a tape, and they need to listen to the details as closely as they can. Once the tape has finished playing, you're going to ask them questions about the details. If you're able, it would be best to play a very short clip and give them a sample question or two so they get the hang of it.

Now about your tape, simply do one of two things—either record on an audio tape a portion of a news program on the radio, including the weather and traffic reports; or record on a videotape the same thing from a television news pro-

gram. If you show a videotape, you'll want to turn the TV around so it's facing away from the kids when you play it. You want the kids to hear it, but you don't want them to have any visual cues.

After you record a section, play it for yourself a few times and create a list of questions based on minute details of the broadcast. Here are some examples—

- On which freeway was the accident with the overturned pickup truck?
- What was the first name of the reporter who told the story about the burglary?
- Fill in this blank: Tonight we'll experience a _____ front in the weather.

Get it? Just make up a dozen questions or so. Kids will most likely get into this game. So if you have time, you could play two or three rounds with different sound clips.

After you ask the question, give the teams 30 seconds to discuss their answer and write it down on a piece of paper. Then reveal the correct answer. Consider giving out some kind of prize to the team that gets the most correct answers.

OPTIONAL GAME
Listen Lists

If you can't pull off that first idea (because you have no way to record sound clips or else you're reading this lesson for the first time at a stoplight

You'll need—

- a few pieces of paper and pens (one for each team)
- an audio cassette or videotape of dialogue recorded from a radio or television news program
- a way to play it for your group
- a list of questions (described below)
- (optional) a bag of candy or some other prize for the winning team

You'll need—
- a few pieces of paper and pens (one for each group)
- (optional) a food prize for the winning team

on the way to youth group), here's another one that needs no preparation. If you have lots of time, you could play both games using the same teams.

Divide your group into teams of three to eight (depending on the size of your group). Tell the teams they're going to compete in a listening competition. You're going to read a list of items then ask a question about it. They'll have about 30 seconds to come up with one group answer and write it down. Make sure they know they're not allowed to write anything down while you're reading the list.

Here are the lists and questions.

1. I'm going to read you a list of articles of clothing. Listen carefully: boots, sweater, belt, cap, bra, pants, vest, Bermuda shorts, socks, jacket, beanie. How many of those items began with the letter B? [five—boots, belt, bra, Bermuda shorts, beanie]

2. I'm going to read you a list of pizza toppings. Listen carefully: onions, pepperoni, pineapple, sausage, olives, green pepper, mushrooms, anchovies, ham, bacon, hamburger. What was the fifth topping on the list? [olives]

3. I'm going to read you a list of toys. Listen carefully: electric train, remote-control car, Barbie doll, Gameboy, Lego blocks, Chutes and Ladders game, sounds and lights keyboard, tea set, Tonka truck, See and Say, Matchbox cars, Beanie Babies. How many of those toys require batteries? [three—remote-control car, Gameboy, sounds and lights keyboard]

4. I'm going to read you a list of names. Listen carefully: Jennifer, Robin, Teresa, Claude, Penelope, Ken, Jim, Peter, Francesca, Tobin, Frank, Connor, Lisa, Brenna. How many of those names have only two syllables? [six—Robin, Peter, Tobin, Connor, Lisa, Brenna]

5. I'm going to read you a list of ice cream flavors. Listen carefully: tutti-fruitti, vanilla, raspberry sherbet, rocky road, chocolate chunk, strawberry swirl, pistachio, lemon ice, chocolate mint, chocolate chip cookie dough. **What was the fourth flavor?** [rocky road]

After your games are over, lead a discussion on listening using these questions as a starting point—

- **Why is listening important?**
- **How can *not listening* cause problems for you?**
- **Why is being a good listener such an important quality in a friend?**
- **Why is it so hard to be a good listener?**

Rebus Verses

Pass out copies of **Rebus Verses** (page 69) and pens or pencils to each kid. Tell them there are two Bible verses on this page and

He's a Big God

Young teens have acquired new word-processing software, so to speak, and they're trying to convert their last ten years' worth of accumulated files into a new format. Young teens are reformatting their files about God, salvation, grace, the Incarnation, and almost every other spiritual topic. They're also reformatting the input from their parents' faith in order to form their own spiritual identities.

My contention is that young teens *must* reenlist in the faith in the same way a soldier recommits to the army. If young teens don't internalize their faith, making it their own, their faith will stagnate by their middle teen years.

Help parents enjoy their teen's doubts and questions. When a parent reports with anguish that their kid has just said, "I'm not sure I want to be a Christian anymore," I always respond by saying, "That's excellent!" After I explain why, their look of shock always melts into relief.

Help kids question their faith. Force them to think in new ways. Enjoy this process.

From *Help! I'm a Junior High Youth Worker!* by Mark Oestreicher (Youth Specialties).

it's their job to decode them. If they've never done a rebus before, simply instruct them to sound out the pictures and follow the instructions until they think they know the word. Give them an example: a picture of a bee plus the number four would be the word *before*. Now give them five or more minutes to solve the rebuses. Some kids will be very quick at this, while others won't quite get it. Move around the room to help those who get stuck.

After kids are done (or thoroughly frustrated!), pull them back together and walk through the answer one word at a time, allowing kids the opportunity to shout out the right word. The first rebus says, "Before they call I will answer; while they are speaking, I will hear." The second rebus reads, "The eyes of the Lord are on the righteous and his ears are attentive to their cry."

After you've gone through the verses word-for-word, read them over again for understanding.

Then ask—

• **Do you believe God listens to us? Why or why not?**
• **How do you think he listens to us?**
• **What difference does it make that he listens to us?**

Self-portrait

How Hard?

Have everyone stand up. Tell them you're going to read some listening situations. Before your group meets, tape one sign that says REALLY HARD and another sign that says NOT HARD AT ALL high up on opposite walls. Point these out to your group now. Tell them that after you read each item, they should move to one of

the walls or somewhere in between to show how hard or easy it would be for them to listen in that situation.

Then read this list and pause for kids to respond by moving.

• **You're watching your favorite TV show and your little brother wants to tell you about his pretend pet.**
• **A close friend of yours is telling you a funny story; and you have one you want to share, but hers is really long.**
• **Your mom is telling you about her junior high school, but you have to go to the bathroom really badly.**
• **Some kid from school starts telling you what he did this past weekend. You really don't want to be seen with him.**
• **A friend of yours is cautiously telling you about something you do that bugs him.**
• **A friend is telling you why she's been kind of bummed lately, but she's really whiny and her story is boring and stupid.**
• **An old guy in your church is trying to tell you about the old days, but your friends are waiting for you down the hall.**
• **A kid you know from school is telling you a great story, but he's really close and has the worst breath you've ever smelled!**

Before you let them go back to their seats, ask, **How good a listener are you, really?** Point to one wall and declare it the I'm-a-fantastic-listener wall. Point to the opposite wall and declare it the I'm-an-awful-listener wall. Have your kids move one more time to register their answers.

Then have everyone return to their seats and continue your discussion on listening with these questions—

• **How does it make people feel when we listen to them?**
• **Who do you know that's a great listener? What do they do that's so great?**
• **How can you improve as a listener?**

Print it!

Listening Practice

Have your kids pair up and stand facing each other. Tell them to choose a talker and a listener. Tell the talkers that when you say, "Go!" you want them to describe one of their favorite vacations in detail. The listeners should listen carefully so they can try to repeat it back.

You'll need—
• music to play
• a few other adult helpers

As soon as you say, "Go," surprise the kids by creating an awful environment for listening: Play loud music. You and a couple other adults start shouting things to each other. Walk through the room and accidentally bump into kids and knock over chairs. Then, suddenly, stop the commotion and the exercise. Now ask the listeners to repeat back to the talkers what they heard.

Ask—

• **Was it hard to listen? Why or why not?**
• **What needed to change in order for you to listen better?**
• **If the music and distractions didn't change, what could you have done to listen better?**

I'm Listening

Wrap up your time by challenging the kids to be gutsy. Tell them you're going to play some background music or a video. While that's going on,

You'll need—
• background music or a music video

you want them to consider taking a gutsy step. They should consider if there's someone in the room for whom they've not been a good listener. Encourage them that if they can think of anyone, they should get up, walk to the person, and tell them, "I'm going to be a better listener." Then they can sit down or tell another person in the room.

First spend a minute in silent prayer, asking God to remind you of whom, if anyone, you should speak with. Then start the background music or video and challenge them to do it. Now, realistically, kids won't jump right up and do this. For the success of this application, it's very important that you and the other adult leaders jump into action and lead the way by modeling. Intentionally choose kids you struggle to listen to. Choose lonely kids that no one else would approach. (You don't want this to turn into some kind of a popularity thing.)

After a few minutes, turn the music or video off and close your time in prayer, thanking God for being such a great listener.

HANDY REVIEW OPTION
Weekly Wall Art

If you're using the signs idea described at the end of Lesson 1, add a graphic of a big ear to your wall.

Rebus Verses

These are pictures puzzles. Say the pictures to yourself, follow the directions, and you'll figure out the words.

 + 4   T+ 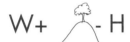 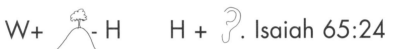 W+ -H

 + sir ;   Y + L   TH+  R -T

 W+ 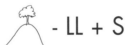 -H   H + . Isaiah 65:24

---

the   ♡ -L the **LORD** R -D

the + -T + D -LL + S

R   A + + IVE   2   TH+ . Psalm 34:15

God is like a COMEDIAN

Our mouths were filled with laughter, our tongues with songs of joy.

Psalm 126:2a

GOALS

Students will—

- Understand why God is like a comedian
- Understand how they can be like a comedian and use humor in good and profitable ways or in destructive ways
- Plan a party to celebrate God's gifts of laughter and fun

Picture Prep

Funny Stuff!

A couple days before your group meets, spend a few minutes at your local video rental store and choose three to five movies that have a really funny scene in them. Think like a junior higher. (Ooh, that could be very, very scary!) *Funny* to a junior higher is not subtle. *Funny* to a junior higher is fast and physical. This is especially true when the viewers (young teens, in this case) don't know the context of the scene. So, pick scenes with slapstick physical comedy in them. I'll give you a handful of suggestions, but you've got to make a deal with me: watch them before you show them to your kids! *Always do this!* Never assume that a recommended video clip is appropriate for your kids, your church, or you! And if you're offended by any of these—*just don't use them!* No need to write nasty letters to me, okay? With your promise, I make the following suggestions.

You'll need—
- three or four laugh-out-loud funny scenes from movies on video
- TV
- VCR

- A great scene from a mediocre comedy called *The Money Pit*, starring Shelly Long and Tom Hanks. After their house has been completely destroyed by workers, there's one hilarious scene with almost no dialogue. It starts as Tom Hanks speaks to one of the workers about a lawsuit against Bob Hope, and ends, a few minutes of catastrophe later, with Tom Hanks in a fountain.
- The dead dog scene from *There's Something About Mary*. No, I don't recommend you show this whole movie to your kids. (Relax—if it makes you feel better, stop the video and say in a loud commanding voice, "I am not suggesting you watch this movie!") But the scene is side-splittingly funny.
- Throw in the short scene from *Austin Powers* (starring Mike Meyers) where Dr. Evil and his cohorts make a major threat to the world powers and then stand there laughing—way too long. It's a bit more subtle but still very funny. If you have any way to edit this stuff onto one tape, it would be great to show a bit of this segment between the other clips.
- Rent *Saturday Night Live Goes Commercial* (larger video stores would have this) and choose one or two of the cleaner fake commercials.
- The "can" scene from Steve Martin's classic comedy *The Jerk*. It's near the beginning. A hit man is trying to kill Steve Martin, who's working at a gas station, but Martin assumes the man hates cans and is shooting any can in sight.

• Or maybe something from *Little Women*—now that was a funny, funny movie. (I'm kidding!)

After you've shown the clips, have kids vote for the one they thought was the funniest.

OPTIONAL GAME
Make Me Laugh

Reenact this great game show from the '80s. (Actually, there's a new version of it on cable, but it will probably be cancelled long before you read this!) It's quite simple: have a volunteer laugher sit in a chair or on a stool (it's better if the audience can see their face) while the three volunteer comedians take 60-second turns trying to make the person laugh or smile. The laugher must look at the comedian—they can't try to tune them out—but cannot laugh or even crack a smile. The comedian's task is to make the laugher smile or laugh without touching them.

Admittedly, most teens aren't funny enough to pull this off; but it's fun just to watch them try! The game is even better, however, if you do one of two things. Either choose goofy and funny kids as the comedians—kids you know will try almost anything to get a laugh—or get a few funny adults who would be willing to spend 20 minutes in your junior high room. And give them the hint that they should be very physical—laugh, fall down, flail around, etc.

Play three rounds. Each round uses all three comedians back-to-back for 60 seconds each. And every round has a new laugher. Enlist the rest of your students to help you watch the laugher to see if she smiles at all. Any laugher who makes it through all three comedians without cracking a smile wins. Consider giving them some small prize if they make it.

After the game is over, ask these questions—

• **What makes you laugh?**
• **What's a funny scene from a movie you've seen recently?**
• **Have you had anything really funny happen to you lately?** (Have a few kids share, if they have stories.)
• **What makes something funny?**

You'll need—
• one chair
• three volunteer laughers (try to get giggly kids for this)
• three volunteer comedians
• (optional) a small candy prize for the laughers who don't laugh

Turn or Burn

When you explain the gospel for evangelistic or outreach purposes, consider these common sense pointers:

• **Remember that it's God's job to change lives, not yours.** Take the pressure off yourself and your audience. Relax. Share the Good News of Jesus Christ. Offer kids an appropriate way to respond and don't sweat the results.
• **Be age-appropriate.** Distill the truth of the Gospel into concepts young teens can grasp. At a recent outreach event, I used the bridge illustration (popularized decades ago by Campus Crusade for Christ's "Four Spiritual Laws") with a stuffed dinosaur as the person, uh, creature trying to get to God.
• **Use stories.** Personal illustrations, contemporary parables, paraphrased Bible stories. Stick with narratives, and kids will stick with you.
• **Follow up.** A clear sign of manipulative evangelism is conversion with no follow-up. If you have students who decide to walk with Christ, fulfill the whole Great Commission (not just the evangelism part) by *making disciples*.

From *Help! I'm a Junior High Youth Worker!* by Mark Oestreicher (Youth Specialties).

Action shot

God's Funny Stuff

Pass out copies of **God's Funny Stuff** (pages 75-76) and pens or pencils to your students. (I like handouts, but I know you might not. If you're so inclined, this would be an easy sheet to

You'll need—
• copies of **God's Funny Stuff** (pages 75-76)
• pens or pencils
• Bibles

go over with the kids verbally, instead of handing it out.) Allow your kids to work in pairs on this one. I'd suggest you give them a couple minutes to complete only part one, then debrief it. Then have them do part two and debrief, and, finally, the last (silly) question. This allows them to stay focused on the task at hand. I realize that *focus* and *junior high group* may seem like mutually exclusive terms at times.

After you're finished with the wildpage, ask, **Can anyone think of something funny that happened in the Bible?** (There's almost no way to predict what answers you'll get for this one—unless you know your group is not familiar with the Bible, in which case you shouldn't ask this question anyway!)

Use the following funny stories as mini, spontaneous melodramas. Have a team of a few actors come up and play the parts as you read them. If there are lines, they can just repeat them after you. Make sure they ham it up and get goofy!

- **Balaam's donkey speaking to him— Numbers 22**
- **Sarah being told she'd have a kid at 80 years old—Genesis 18**
- **Absalom gets his hair caught in a tree and is left hanging—2 Samuel 18**
- **Aaron saying the golden calf just walked out of the fire—Exodus 32**
- **Frightened, little wimpy Gideon being addressed by God's angel as a mighty warrior—Judges 6**
- **Eutychus gets preached to death—Acts 20**

Wrap up this section with a discussion around this question: **Why do you think God created humor?** *[Let the kids struggle to come up with answers for a bit. Just like all good things— food, sex, fellowship—God made humor to build us up and add joy to our lives. Humor may not serve as useful a function as food or sex, but the fact that God created humor is added proof of his love for us. He wants our lives to be filled with joy!]*

Self-portrait

Humor Vote

Make a transition by saying something like, **God made humor and laughter and fun. He really wants you to enjoy life, have fun, and laugh. But—just like all the good stuff God created—Satan has distorted it and made it into something that can also be bad. Bad or destructive humor— humor that displeases God—can look a lot like good humor. It still makes you laugh. It's still fun. So we have to be extra careful that the humor we use and enjoy is what God intended for our own good, not what Satan ruined.**

You'll need—
• one copy of **Humor Vote** (page 77) for you to read

Pull out your copy of **Humor Vote** (page 77) and tell your group you're going to read several situations where kids are laughing and having fun. After each story, stop and ask your kids to vote whether the humor and laughter in the story was God-stuff (uplifting) or Satan-stuff (hurtful or sinful). They are to register their votes in this manner—

- **For a God-stuff vote, they should pretend to be laughing uncontrollably.**
- **For a Satan-stuff vote, they should groan like they would after a bad joke.**

After each vote, ask kids to justify their answers. Some of the situations don't have obvious answers—like the one about uncontrollable giggling in church. Kids will assume that you think this is bad because it takes place in church, but what's really wrong about it? Help them to think critically about whether or not the situation is a corruption of how God intended humor to be. I've given you my opinion in parentheses after each story—don't read these to your kids.

After you've read the stories, called for the votes, and discussed them, lead a discussion around this question: **How can you tell if something is God-stuff humor or Satan-stuff humor?** [Asking yourself, "Would it be pleasing to God?" is the main answer to this question. If it makes fun of someone or a group of people or evil stuff—like sex outside of marriage—then it's not good or healthy.]

Party Planning

Say, **Okay, if God wants us to have fun, then we're going to. And you all are going to plan it.**
Announce a party for your group and give the date (one you've already selected).

You'll need—
• paper
• pens

Then tell the kids they're going to plan the party—and they'd better make sure it's fun! If the size of your group is medium or small, have them plan it for the whole group. If you have a larger group, you might consider breaking them into groups and planning smaller parties (maybe a girls' party and a guys' party, or even separate parties for each gender and grade). Have leaders (or yourself) sit in on the planning to encourage (or discourage, as the case may be) the planning. But allow them to come up with the actual ideas. You may need to prod their thinking with some questions (Should we go somewhere? Should we eat anything?).

Close your time by thanking God for creating laughter and fun, and by asking for wisdom to tell the difference between the kind of joking around that pleases him and the kind that doesn't.

HANDY REVIEW OPTION
Weekly Wall Art

If you're using the signs idea described at the end of Lesson 1, add a graphic to your wall of a large, laughing mouth.

God's Funny Stuff

Part 1
God's Funny Creations

Can you believe God created these things? Rate each of these on the funny creation scale below it.

Dogs chasing their own tails

ha   ha-ha   HA-HA!   HA-HA-HOO-HEE-HEE!

Loud uncontrolled burps

ha   ha-ha   HA-HA!   HA-HA-HOO-HEE-HEE!

Monkeys swinging in trees

ha   ha-ha   HA-HA!   HA-HA-HOO-HEE-HEE!

Those little lizards that can run on water

ha   ha-ha   HA-HA!   HA-HA-HOO-HEE-HEE!

How milk will shoot out your nose if you laugh with a mouthful

ha   ha-ha   HA-HA!   HA-HA-HOO-HEE-HEE!

The sound (God created it!) of passing gas

ha   ha-ha   HA-HA!   HA-HA-HOO-HEE-HEE!

God's Funny Stuff

Part 2
Multiple-Choice Laughing Verses

Choose the right verse below each reference. Look them up for the right answers.

Psalm 126:2a
____ Our mouths were filled with laughter, our tongues with songs of joy.
____ Our mouths were filled with peanut butter, and our tongues were stuck.
____ Our mouths were filled with joy, and you gave us nice songs to sing.

Job 8:21
____ God will make you happy, and you'll want to tell him so.
____ He will yet fill your mouth with laughter and your lips with shouts of joy.
____ He will fill your mouth with marshmallow fluff, and your lips will spew little chunks of it.

Ecclesiastes 3:1a, 4a
____ There is a time for everything … a time to be sad and a time to be happy.
____ There is a time for everything … a time to giggle and a time to guffaw.
____ There is a time for everything … a time to weep and a time to laugh.

Part 3
A Final Question

Do you think God has a sense of humor?

❏ yes

❏ no

❏ uh …

76

Humor Vote

Julia and Brianne are eating lunch in the school cafeteria. Julia is taking a big sip of Coke right when Brianne says something funny. Julia tries to swallow but just can't. She ends up spraying the Coke all over Brianne, and they both start laughing uncontrollably. *[Good stuff—just like God wants humor to be!]*

Phil, Kirby, and Scott are walking home from school together, and they're killing time by telling jokes. Kirby's got a whole list of funny jokes he heard from his uncle about gay people. The three guys laughed so hard they thought they were going to be sick. *[Bad stuff—hurtful to a group of people and probably sexual in nature.]*

Gretchen, Kelly, Jeff, and Terrance are working on a science experiment together. Gretchen, Kelly, and Terrance are popular kids who hang out together all the time. Jeff is not popular at all—in fact he's kind of a science geek. Jeff reaches out to grab some part of their experiment and accidentally burns his hand on the flame. Terrance says, "What a dork!" and the three of them bust out laughing. Jeff kind of laughs along also. *[Bad stuff—hurtful to Jeff even though he's laughing.]*

Rita and Karen are sitting in church, and they're actually paying attention. But when the pastor was making announcements, he accidentally said, "Come to our *pig* celebration," instead of "Come to our *big* celebration." It wasn't that funny, but Rita and Karen couldn't stop giggling. They tried their hardest to stop, but knowing they weren't supposed to be laughing only made it worse. *[Good stuff—innocent laughter.]*

Billy and his grandma were watching the old movie *Back to the Future*. A guy in the movie lost control of his convertible and it slid into the back of a dump truck filled with cow manure, which dumped all over him and filled up his car. Billy started laughing right out loud, but his grandma said, "I don't see what's funny about that at all." *[Good stuff—just a silly scene with no evil intentions.]*

When Gina picked up the phone, it was Lydia and Vicki three-way calling her. Lydia and Vicki were giggling like crazy and told her the funniest piece of gossip about this girl in their school. Gina thought it was funny too, and they all laughed and talked about whom they should call next. *[Bad stuff—gossip humor.]*

77

God is like a CHILD

Therefore, whoever humbles himself like this child is the greatest in the kingdom of heaven. Matthew 18:4

Students will—

• Understand why God is like a child
• Understand how they can be like a child by loving God with a pure and uncompromising faith
• Choose two childlike faith characteristics to incorporate into their own lives.

Picture Prep

Kid-Words

Play your own version of the board game *Scattergories*. Divide your group into teams of three to eight kids each. Give each team a piece of paper and a pen or pencil, and instruct them to appoint a scribe—someone to write for their group.

Tell them that in a few minutes you're going to give them a letter of the alphabet. Their team's job is to come up with as many words or items as possible that begin with that letter, *but which also have some connection to little kids or babies.*

Offer this example, **If I said the letter was B, you might come up with boy, baby, boogers, booties, Barbie dolls, and bedtime.**

While they want to think of as many words as possible, their real goal is to come up with words that the other teams don't have on their lists. Therefore, they should work quietly so the other teams won't hear them.

After you give a letter, allow about 60 seconds for them to generate words and write them down. Then have a group share their answers. Anytime another group has the same word, they must shout out that they have it. Then both groups (and any other group with that word) must cross it off their lists. Have other groups read their remaining words. Groups only get points for words that no other group has on their list. By the way, you have to act as an impartial judge and rule on whether or not words are really associated with kids and babies. They're not allowed to use adjectives that start with *B* in order to make a phrase that meets the requirements. For example, they couldn't use *blue toys* as a *B* word. *T, S, R, M,* and *L* are all good letters to use.

After the game is over, total up the teams' scores and consider giving a prize to the winning team.

Then ask—

• **What are some things that make little kids different from you?**
• **What words would you use to describe a little kid's emotions?**
• **What words would you use to describe a little kid's behavior?**
• **What words would you use to describe how a little kid believes in God?**

You'll need—

• one piece of paper
• pen or pencil for every three to eight kids
• (optional) a bag of candy or some other prize for the winning team

- **What's not complete about the way little kids think about God?**
- **What's good about the way little kids think about God?**

Action shot

Kid Jesus Dramas

Continue your questions and make a transition with these (ask kids to explain their answers on all of these)—

- **What do you think Jesus was like as a little kid? Was he a goody-goody?**
- **Do you think he ever got in trouble?**
- **Do you think he ever ticked off his brothers and sisters?**
- **Do you think he liked school?**
- **Do you think he got hurt or sick?**
- **Do you think he played sports?**
- **Do you think he had dreams like you?**

Now tell your kids they're going to create short dramas about what Jesus might have been like as a kid. Divide them into three groups (if you have a large group, you could use six groups).

Give one of the strips you've cut from the top half of **Kid Jesus Dramas** (page 82) to each group. Each strip instructs the group to take a different direction with their treatment of Kid Jesus. Then give them about five to seven minutes to create their dramas. It would be best (big time!) if you had an adult in each group to help them.

Each slip has the group reflect a different kind of Kid Jesus. The first two are false perceptions,

though very common, of what Jesus would have been like—either a serious party-pooper or a wimpy little cheesepuff. The last drama *should* (ah, the joys of junior high work—who knows what will really happen?) reflect a more accurate Jesus—a real kid!

After all three teams have performed their dramas, ask everyone to vote for the one that probably reflects what Jesus was really like. (Hopefully, they'll choose the third one!) Ask for reasons why they chose that one (or whichever one they chose) and not the others.

Then show your kids one of the only verses that says anything about Jesus' childhood—Luke 2:40. "And the child grew and became strong; he was filled with wisdom, and the grace of God was upon him." (Of course, there's also the story of 12-year-old Jesus in the temple, but since some of your kids are 12, it doesn't suit our purposes to consider that age group to be within our definition of *kid*.)

Ask what they think the verse means when it says Jesus was "filled with wisdom."

Next, turn a little corner by saying something like, **Okay, we don't know a whole lot about Jesus' childhood—but we *do* know what he thinks about kids!**

Send your kids back to their drama teams and assign each of them a set of passages that

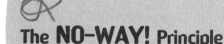

The NO-WAY! Principle

Every now and then it's worth it to put in the time, effort, and money to really blow your kids' minds.

Strong early adolescent ministry creates memories. Some of these need to be the kind that inspire kids to say, "I can't believe we did that! I could never do this anywhere else!"

That's the No Way! Principle.

Create a No Way! sense of awe and excitement on different scales. Make your students gasp "Wow!" by throwing handfuls of candy at them. Or create an event—games and all—around raw fish or Cornish hens (while still frozen, the latter work great for bowling down a tiled church hallway). Sponsor a swim party where everyone enters the pool fully dressed. Cover the floor of your room with a foot of shredded foam rubber.

It can be just as mind-blowing to kids for you to stop in the middle of a lesson and ask them to turn their handouts into paper airplanes.

You'll find lots of No Way! ideas in *Memory Makers* by Doug Fields and Duffy Robbins (Youth Specialties).

From Help! I'm a Junior High Youth Worker! *by Mark Oestreicher (Youth Specialties).*

are listed on the slips you've cut apart from the *bottom* half of **Kid Jesus Dramas.**

Luke 18:15-17 and Matthew 18:1-6
Mark 10:13-16 and Matthew 18:1-6
Matthew 19:13-15 and Matthew 18:1-6

Ask them to look at the passage together, then answer this question, **What is it about children that Jesus praises?** *[Their faith.]* Follow up by asking: **What about their faith does Jesus like?** *[It's simple and pure and wild and adventurous.]*

OPTIONAL VIDEO
Witnesses

Get a copy of Curt Cloninger's video *Witnesses* and show the monologue of Zirim the tailor, a fictitious character who knew Jesus as a child. It's a powerful piece that will hold your kids' attention.

Wild or Safe?

Distribute copies of **Wild or Safe** (pages 83-84) and pens or pencils to your kids. Have them work on their own to complete the first section, then talk about it. Do the same with the second and third sections. The point of this wildpage is to flesh out the fact that a child's faith (the faith that Jesus praises and desires us to have) is wild, sold-out,

You'll need—
• copies of **Wild or Safe** (pages 83-84)
• pens or pencils

uncompromising, and pure.

After they've finished the sheet, ask, **Why is it hard to have this kind of faith sometimes?** *[It's natural to*

have doubts and struggles as we grow up, and they're not all bad. While God certainly wants junior highers to wrestle with their faith and make it their own, he still longs for all of us to have a pure and fresh faith.]

Faith Step

Finally, have your students look at the words in the left column on the last question of that wildpage. Ask them to take a minute and circle two words they would like to use when describing their own faith in God.

Now ask them to turn their sheets over and, on the blank back side, write down a few ideas for how they might go about making those faith descriptions a reality in their lives. Admittedly, this will be pretty tough for many of your kids, especially those with simplistic, childlike thinking abilities. If you use small groups at all, this would be an ideal place to use them—that way an adult and other peers can help kids brainstorm ways to make this a reality. If you don't use small groups (what are you thinking?), go ahead and have kids get into groups of two or three and work together to come up with ideas. Or if your group is small enough (six or fewer kids), you could just go through each student's answers as a group.

Wrap up your time by having everyone spend a few moments praying silently that God would help them grow in that area of their faith.

You'll need—
• the wildpage you just finished!

HANDY REVIEW OPTION
Weekly Wall Art

If you're using the signs idea described at the end of Lesson 1, add a big graphic to your wall of a kid.

Kid Jesus Dramas

1 Your group is to come up with a short drama using any situation you choose, but the characters are to be Jesus as an eight-year-old and some other eight-year-olds. (They could be his group of friends, school mates, temple youth group members, or whatever.) Jesus should act real serious and preachy. Have him act more like an 80-year-old man than an eight-year-old boy. Sample Jesus line: "You shouldn't do that!"

2 Your group is to come up with a short drama using any situation you choose, but the characters are to be Jesus as an eight-year-old and some other eight-year-olds. (They could be his group of friends, school mates, temple youth group members, or whatever.) Jesus should be a whiney, wimpy little kid—quicker to quote some Bible verse than to play a game. Sample Jesus line: "I don't want to get dirty!"

3 Your group is to come up with a short drama using any situation you choose, but the characters are to be Jesus as an eight-year-old and some other eight-year-olds. (They could be his group of friends, school mates, temple youth group members, or whatever.) You are to make Jesus act like a real eight-year-old boy—a goofy, restless little kid who loves to play and likes being mischievous. Sample Jesus line, "Let's wrestle!"

1 Luke 18:15-17 and Matthew 18:1-6

2 Mark 10:13-16 and Matthew 18:1-6

3 Matthew 19:13-15 and Matthew 18:1-6

82

Wild or Safe

1. Circle the words below that describe a little kid.

energetic FUN-LOVING educated FIDGETY

quiet calm random

gullible

cultured LOVING IMPULSIVE

RISK-TAKING precise

wild

loud

SAFE

formal trusting messy

APPROPRIATE boogery

2. Now look at the words you just circled. Which one of the following statements best describes a child's faith in God? (circle one)

I think I believe in God. I mean, my parents do. And I guess...I don't know...

God is cool! I don't see why people have all these questions about God. He's God, and I believe him, and that's it!

I have all kinds of doubts. I'm not really sure what I believe. I'm still working it out.

Yeah, I believe in God, but so what? Doesn't everyone?

83

Wild or Safe, part 2

3. Kids are fired up about God! Their faith is total. God is who he says he is. That's it. Subject closed. Circle the list of words below that best describes a child's faith.

wild	controlled
trusting	doubting
pure	muddy
willing	resisting
whole	partial
unfailing	faltering
simple	complex
fresh	boring
complete	reserved

Now go back and put a mark on each line to show where you are in your faith.

God is like a JUDGE

And the heavens proclaim his righteousness, for God himself is judge.

Psalm 50:6

GOALS

Students will—

- Understand why God is like a judge
- Understand how they can be like a judge by making good decisions
- Exercise wisdom to make a decision

Picture Prep

Court Is in Session!

Start your time by telling your group you're going to hold court today. Each of them will be part of a team of lawyers, and you will be the judge.

Here's how it works. I've given you a list of six charges (page 89). Each of these will act like a different case, but you don't have to do them all. If your group is a dozen or less kids, just do a couple of them. But if your group is larger or if you have lots of time to kill, feel free to use 'em all.

You'll divide your group into legal teams—a prosecution team and a defense team—for each case. So if you're planning on using two of the cases, you'll need four legal teams. Get it? It's not advanced math! So divide your kids into teams and hand

You'll need—

- a few copies of **The Charges** (page 89)
- one copy of **The Sentences** (page 90), cut into strips
- a chair and table for the judge's bench
- a hammer for a gavel
- (optional) a black robe would add a nice touch!

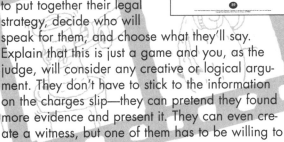

them a copy of their case. Make sure you explain whether they're the defense team or the prosecution team—and explain what that means.

Tell the teams they'll have about three minutes to put together their legal strategy, decide who will speak for them, and choose what they'll say. Explain that this is just a game and you, as the judge, will consider any creative or logical argument. They don't have to stick to the information on the charges slip—they can pretend they found more evidence and present it. They can even create a witness, but one of them has to be willing to play that part.

Now all you need are defendants. Basically, you just need to pick them. Read the charges to yourself beforehand and choose kids that will play along. You don't need to ask them to volunteer—just call them out at the beginning of the trial. It would be best if they weren't on one of the legal teams for that particular case. But if they are, it's not a big deal.

After the legal teams have had a few minutes to put together their strategy, call out the first case. The legal teams can move to the front if they want. Then announce the name of the defendant and have him come sit with the defenders.

After you read the charges, allow the prosecution about three to five minutes to present their case. They can call the defendant as a witness, if they'd like. Then allow the defense team the same amount of time.

After the arguments are complete, announce your verdict. Choose your verdict based on which team presented a more compelling case. Don't get hung up on *truth* or anything like that!

If the verdict is guilty, have the defendant come forward and blindly choose one of the sentencing slips you've cut apart (page 90). Have him perform the sentence right then and there. Then move on to the next case on your docket.

After all the cases have been tried, ask these questions—

- **What kind of judge was I? Did I seem fair?**
- **What's the job of a judge?** [To discern the truth and make decisions.]
- **What makes a good judge?** [One who makes good and fair decisions.]

Judge God

Lead your students through a paraphrase of Matthew 25:31-46 with a spontaneous melodrama (page 91). You'll need to get kids to act out the parts, but they don't have to learn any lines. They just have to be willing to ham it up as you read the action. Instruct them that if their character has any lines, they should just repeat them after you. This melodrama, in particular, will be very easy for kids to be a part of, since most of the performers will be acting in a group. Make sure you

You'll need—
- one copy of the **Judge God Melodrama** (page 91) for you to read
- a bunch of volunteers
- Bibles

read the script through prior to your group time so you can read it well and with appropriate story-telling flair.

After you've acted out this Academy Award-winning script (well, the award is still pending), have your students turn in their Bibles to Matthew 25:31-46. Read the passage to them. Then ask—

- **Who are the goats? What kind of person is this?**
- **Who are the sheep? What kind of people are they?**
- **You just saw God the Judge in action. What do you think of his verdict?**
- **How did he come to his decision?**

Have your kids look at a couple of verses—

And the heavens proclaim his righteousness, for God himself is judge. (Psalm 50:6)

Many seek an audience with a ruler, but it is from the Lord that man gets justice. (Proverbs 29:26)

Say something like, **God is the ultimate judge because he never has to figure out right or wrong, and he never has to guess at what's fair. He already knows.**

Self-portrait

A Bunch of Judges

Make a transition by asking, **How can we be like judges?** [Kids will probably answer something like, "When we make a decision for other people," or something involving other people, since they'll think of a courtroom. But the answer is simply that we're like judges when we make good decisions. But don't worry about revealing the complete answer at this point.]

Now pass out copies of **A Bunch of Judges** (page 92) and pens or pencils to each kid. Allow them to work in pairs or groups of three. They need to read the five short stories and order them from one to five. Number five should be the student who is most like a judge, and number one should be the student who is least like a judge. You might want to read all five stories out loud, so they can begin the ordering

process at the same time. Otherwise some kids will be all done by the time others are just finishing the first story! Then give them a little time to complete the ordering.

After a few minutes, get feedback. If your group is small, you can have them share their opinions. But if your group is larger, ask how many rated the first story as the most judge-like, then the second story, and so on. Do the same thing for the least judge-like.

Then ask, **Now that you've looked at these examples, what does it take for you to be judge-like? Does it have to involve other people? Can you be judge-like just by making a good decision?**

Continue with these questions—

• **How do you make good decisions?** [Consider the options, think about different outcomes, pray, ask for advice.]
• **How do you know if it's a good decision?**
• **If you know how to make good decisions, why do you make bad ones sometimes?** [Sometimes we make bad decisions because we want what the bad decision offers us, even though we know it's not the best for us in the long run.]

Print it!

Make a Choice

Ask your students to turn their papers over and use the blank side. Tell them to take a minute and think of a decision they have to make in the next few weeks. It can be something really big, like which parent to live with or whether to hang with a certain group of friends. Or it could be something much simpler, like what class to take at school or whether or not to keep

87

their paper route. After they think of something, they should write it down at the top of the paper.

Have a few kids share their undecided decisions. Then ask them to spend a minute writing the different choices they have. For some decisions this will be extremely simple; but for others, it will take some thought.

Now tell them they don't have to write them down, but you want them to think of the consequences of the different choices they've written down.

Pause for a minute of prayer, asking God to give everyone guidance. Now suggest that if they're willing, they should circle one of the possible answers and make a good judge-like decision right now.

Close your group in prayer, asking God for wisdom to make good decisions.

HANDY REVIEW OPTION
Weekly Wall Art

If you're using the signs idea described in Lesson 1, add a large graphic of a judge's gavel to your wall. Don't forget to review the other images with your kids to remind them of the other God pictures you talked about.

The Charges

- ✂- - -

The defendant is charged with theft. The charges state that the defendant's little sister had just opened a lollipop when the defendant stole it right out of her hands and ate it.

- ✂- - -

The defendant is charged with gossip. The charges state that the defendant's friend shared a rumor about another kid in school, and the defendant passed it on to 43 other students.

- ✂- - -

The defendant is charged with whining. The charges state that the defendant's parents asked the defendant to clean her room. Allegedly, the defendant proceeded to whine and complain.

- ✂- - -

The defendant is charged with telling stupid jokes. The charges state that the defendant continually tells the most annoying jokes in the world.

- ✂- - -

The defendant is charged with puking on a friend. The charges state that, while the defendant was truly sick and needed to vomit, the defendant showed no discretion in the placement of the stream of vomit, thereby soaking the defendant's friend.

- ✂- - -

The defendant is charged with excessive bathroom time. The multiple charges state that the defendant leaves the junior high group at church to go to the bathroom all the time. In addition, the defendant's sister alleges that the defendant hogs the bathroom every morning before school.

- ✂- - -

89

COURT IS IN SESSION!
The Sentences

- ✂

Your sentence is—

You must sing the National Anthem, right now.

- ✂

Your sentence is—

You must act like a chicken for 15 seconds, right now.

- ✂

Your sentence is—

You must shout, "I'm a crazy woman [or man] five times, right now.

- ✂

Your sentence is—

You must make up a poem about yourself, right now.

- ✂

Your sentence is—

You must perform a short rap about the case against you, right now.

- ✂

Your sentence is—

You must disco dance for 15 seconds, right now.

- ✂

Your sentence is—

You must grab someone by the shoulders and yell, "The world is ending!" right now.

- ✂

Your sentence is—

You must sing "It's a Small World," right now.

- ✂

Your sentence is—

You must pretend to be a mime, right now.

- ✂

Your sentence is—

You must pretend to be the Hunchback of Notre Dame, right now.

- ✂

Judge God Melodrama

Characters
- *God the Judge*
- *Group of goody-goodies (three to five kids)*
- *Group of everyday Christians (three to five kids)*

One day God was walking around heaven, and he said to himself, "I think I'll call a meeting." So he did. He invited all the goody-goodies and all the everyday Christians.

The goody-goodies said in their sweet, little, perfect voices, "We're here, God. *(pause)* We know you love us the best, *(pause)* because we're so go-o-o-d."

The everyday Christians also said, "Here we are, God. *(pause)* Thanks for inviting us."

God boomed, "goody-goodies stand over there," and he pointed to one side. Then he pointed to another space and said nicely, "everyday Christians, please stand over there."

The goody-goodies turned their noses up in the air, smiled, and said, "This is wonderful! *(pause)* We're sure glad we don't have to stand with *those* people."

Then God turned to the goody-goodies and said, "Bummer for you! *(pause)* You will have to be separated from me!" At this, the goody-goodies all gasped loudly and continued gasping over and over again. God continued, "You ignored me when I was hungry, *(pause)* you stuck your noses in the air when I was thirsty, *(pause)* you laughed when I didn't have clothes, *(pause)* and you forgot about me when I was in prison."

The goody-goodies were still gasping. Then they said, "But— *(pause)* but— *(pause)* but— *(pause)* we never saw you hungry *(pause)* or thirsty *(pause)* or naked *(pause)*. And we didn't know you were in prison!" *(pause)*

God answered, "However you treated people in these situations, *(pause)* you were treating me! Now go!"

With that, the goody-goodies started whimpering *(pause)* loudly. A few started crying. They looked down at the ground and slowly shuffled away.

Then God turned to the everyday Christians. He said with a happy voice, "Time to celebrate! *(pause)* Because you fed me when I was hungry, *(pause)* and gave me bottled water when I was thirsty, *(pause)* and gave me clothes when I didn't have enough. *(pause)* You even visited me in prison."

The everyday Christians looked confused. They looked at each other and said, "Huh?" a bunch of times. Then they said to God, "But— *(pause)* but— *(pause)* but— *(pause)* we never saw you hungry *(pause)* or thirsty *(pause)* or naked *(pause)*. And we didn't know you were in prison!"

God answered, "When you took care of people in those situations, *(pause)* you were taking care of me! *(pause)* Let the party begin!"

The everyday Christians started to smile. Then they started jumping for joy! God jumped with them.

End

A Bunch of Judges

Order these students from five to one. Five is the most judge-like; one is the least judge-like.

____ Paige knows what she should do. She's got a major book report due tomorrow, and she's been putting it off all week. Her best friend Carly is having a few kids over tonight to watch a brand new movie out on video. Paige has never seen the movie and would love to watch it with her friends. But even though it just about kills her, she decides to stay home and work on her book report. What a drag.

____ Rachel baby-sits on Mondays after school for the twin boys next door—Cassidy and Carlisle. Today the boys were having a huge fight over who got to play with a certain toy. Rachel tried to get them to share but they wouldn't—they just kept fighting. So Rachel took the toy away and said, "If you guys can't work it out, neither of you get it!"

____ Mike is totally into sports. He plays football, basketball, and baseball. He used to play soccer until he couldn't fit it into his schedule this year. Now he's got a new problem. He's been asked to play on a traveling team for indoor soccer. However, the soccer schedule totally conflicts with his basketball schedule. He really wants to play both. Even though he made the decision to drop soccer this year, he decides to join the traveling team, reasoning that he's not very tall and probably won't go very far in basketball anyway.

____ Kennon can hardly contain his excitement. He bursts into his house and is dying to tell his whole family that he won the art competition at school. But before he can say anything, he sees his sister talking to his mom—and she's crying. Apparently his sister is really bummed because she feels she's not very good at anything. Kennon decides this isn't the best time to share his exciting news. It can wait for later.

____ All Belinda's friends drink alcohol. She's tried it a few times, too; but they're really starting to drink all the time now. Every weekend they figure out how to get stuff and then get drunk. Her dad is an alcoholic; and Belinda has always worried that if she starts to drink, she'll never stop—and she'll end up just like her dad. So she made a really hard decision. She chose to find a new group of friends and stopped hanging out with her old friends, even though she really cares about them.

Resources from Youth Specialties

Professional Resources

Administration, Publicity, & Fundraising (Ideas Library)
Developing Student Leaders
Equipped to Serve: Volunteer Youth Worker Training Course
Help! I'm a Junior High Youth Worker!
Help! I'm a Small-Group Leader!
Help! I'm a Sunday School Teacher!
Help! I'm a Volunteer Youth Worker!
How to Expand Your Youth Ministry
How to Speak to Youth...and Keep Them Awake at the Same Time
Junior High Ministry (Updated & Expanded)
The Ministry of Nurture: A Youth Worker's Guide to Discipling Teenagers
One Kid at a Time: Reaching Youth through Mentoring
Purpose-Driven Youth Ministry
So That's Why I Keep Doing This! 52 Devotional Stories for Youth Workers
A Youth Ministry Crash Course
The Youth Worker's Handbook to Family Ministry

Youth Ministry Programming

Camps, Retreats, Missions, & Service Ideas (Ideas Library)
Compassionate Kids: Practical Ways to Involve Your Students in Mission and Service
Creative Bible Lessons from the Old Testament
Creative Bible Lessons in 1 & 2 Corinthians
Creative Bible Lessons in John: Encounters with Jesus
Creative Bible Lessons in Romans: Faith on Fire!
Creative Bible Lessons on the Life of Christ
Creative Junior High Programs from A to Z, Vol. 1 (A-M)
Creative Junior High Programs from A to Z, Vol. 2 (N-Z)
Creative Meetings, Bible Lessons, & Worship Ideas (Ideas Library)
Crowd Breakers & Mixers (Ideas Library)
Drama, Skits, & Sketches (Ideas Library)
Drama, Skits, & Sketches 2 (Ideas Library)
Dramatic Pauses
Everyday Object Lessons
Facing Your Future: Graduating Youth Group with a Faith That Lasts
Games (Ideas Library)
Games 2 (Ideas Library)
Great Fundraising Ideas for Youth Groups
More Great Fundraising Ideas for Youth Groups
Great Retreats for Youth Groups
Greatest Skits on Earth
Greatest Skits on Earth, Vol. 2
Holiday Ideas (Ideas Library)
Hot Illustrations for Youth Talks
More Hot Illustrations for Youth Talks
Still More Hot Illustrations for Youth Talks
Incredible Questionnaires for Youth Ministry
Junior High Game Nights
More Junior High Game Nights

Kickstarters: 101 Ingenious Intros to Just about Any Bible Lesson
Live the Life! Student Evangelism Training Kit
Memory Makers
Play It! Great Games for Groups
Play It Again! More Great Games for Groups
Special Events (Ideas Library)
Spontaneous Melodramas
Super Sketches for Youth Ministry
Teaching the Bible Creatively
Videos That Teach
What Would Jesus Do? Youth Leader's Kit
Youth Leader's Kit: The Next Level
Wild Truth Bible Lessons
Wild Truth Bible Lessons 2
Wild Truth Bible Lessons—Pictures of God
Worship Services for Youth Groups

Discussion Starters

Discussion & Lesson Starters (Ideas Library)
Discussion & Lesson Starters 2 (Ideas Library)
Get 'Em Talking
Keep 'Em Talking!
High School TalkSheets
More High School TalkSheets
High School TalkSheets: Psalms and Proverbs
Junior High TalkSheets
More Junior High TalkSheets
Junior High TalkSheets: Psalms and Proverbs
What If...? 450 Thought-Provoking Questions to Get Teenagers Talking, Laughing, and Thinking
Would You Rather...? 465 Provocative Questions to Get Teenagers Talking
Have You Ever...? 450 Intriguing Questions Guaranteed to Get Teenagers Talking

Clip Art

ArtSource: Stark Raving Clip Art (print)
ArtSource: Youth Group Activities (print)
ArtSource CD-ROM: Clip Art Library Version 2.0

Videos

EdgeTV
The Heart of Youth Ministry: A Morning with Mike Yaconelli
Next Time I Fall in Love Video Curriculum
Understanding Your Teenager Video Curriculum

Student Books

Grow For It Journal
Grow For It Journal through the Scriptures
Teen Devotional Bible
What Would Jesus Do? Spiritual Challenge Journal
Spiritual Challenge Journal: The Next Level
Wild Truth Journal for Junior Highers
Wild Truth Journal—Pictures of God

At **10 TO 20**, we create media for **ONE PURPOSE**:
TO BROADCAST LIFE'S MOST IMPORTANT MESSAGE INTO THE HEADS AND HEARTS OF TEENAGERS.

production for
promotion, broadcast,
conferences and curriculum

graphics, sound, animation,
and digital video for CD, DVD,
and event presentations

teen books, training materials,
and the Wild Truth line for
junior high students and leaders

event consultation,
programming, production,
and media presentation

If you're in youth ministry, we can help you
broadcast the Message to your students.
CHECK OUT OUR MINISTRY TOOLS AT WWW.10TO20.COM

P.O. Box 604 • Del Mar, CA 92014 • 858-793-8275 • info@10to20.com